D1526742

EARLY WELSH
GNOMIC POEMS

EARLY WELSH GNOMIC POEMS.

Edited by *Hurlstone*
KENNETH JACKSON

SECOND IMPRESSION

CARDIFF
THE UNIVERSITY OF WALES PRESS

FIRST IMPRESSION 1935
SECOND IMPRESSION 1961

PRINTED IN GREAT BRITAIN

CONTENTS

PREFACE

ONE of the most outstanding needs of Celtic scholarship at the present time is critical editions, with commentaries, of the early poetry contained in the famous *Four Ancient Books of Wales*, and it is hoped that this book may be a small contribution towards the study of one section of it. It has its origin in some research on Welsh and Irish nature-poetry undertaken for the Allen Scholarship in 1933–4, so that the gnomic verse edited here consists only of those poems where nature-poetry, whether gnomic or descriptive, is an important element. Apart from their significance in the history of Welsh literature they have an added importance in that, taken together with the exceedingly similar Anglo-Saxon gnomic poetry, they form a valuable illustration of semi-popular philosophy and thought in Britain in the early Middle Ages. The present texts are intended for the use of students in the University of Wales and others who have ready access to the standard Welsh books of reference; and it has been possible to limit the bulk of the notes very considerably in the case of words whose meaning has been established already in, for example, the Bulletin of the Board of Celtic Studies, by giving only the references to them instead of reproducing unnecessarily what has been sufficiently dealt with elsewhere.

I should like to thank my former teachers Professor and Mrs H. M. Chadwick for encouraging me to take up this work; the authorities of the National Library of

Wales, the Bodleian Library, and the British Museum, for kindly giving me facilities for consulting their manuscripts; and the Syndics of the University of Wales Press for undertaking the publication. But above all, my warmest thanks are due to Professor Ifor Williams, who read the whole of the poems with me, for so generously allowing me to take advantage of his time and his profound Welsh scholarship. It would be impossible for me to acknowledge all the passages where, particularly in the Notes, I am so deeply indebted to his assistance, but any student of early Welsh literature will realise that they are very many.

K. J.

Cambridge
May 1935

PREFACE TO
THE SECOND IMPRESSION

THE first impression of this book having been exhausted, the University of Wales Press Board decided that a second impression was needed. In the twenty-five years which have passed some modifications have appeared desirable. Short of a full second edition, it was not possible to incorporate these, and they are given on pp.71ff. below as an *Addenda and Corrigenda* (I wish to thank Professors Henry Lewis and Thomas Jones for some helpful comments which they kindly sent me, which are acknowledged there). In the same way, the complete re-edition of the Englynion y Misoedd which might have been undertaken on the basis of the additional MSS. mentioned on p.17 is not feasible in the present circumstances.

K. J.

Edinburgh
1960

LIST OF ABBREVIATIONS

ACL = Archiv für Celtische Lexicographie.

Anc. Laws = Aneurin Owen, Ancient Laws and Institutes of Wales.

Arch. Brit. = Ed. Lhuyd, Archaeologia Britannica.

Arch. Camb. = Archaeologia Cambrensis.

BA = The Book of Aneirin (references to J. G. Evans' edition, by page and line).

BBC = The Black Book of Carmarthen (references to J. G. Evans' edition, by folio and line).

BBCh. = The Black Book of Chirk.

BBCh. prov. = The proverbs in the Black Book of Chirk (ed. Ifor Williams, Bull. III, p.22).

BT = The Book of Taliessin (references to J. G. Evans' edition, by page and line).

Bull. = The Bulletin of the Board of Celtic Studies.

CLH = Ifor Williams, Canu Llywarch Hen.

Conts. = K. Meyer, Contributions to Irish Lexicography.

Cott. Gn. = The Anglo-Saxon Gnomic Poem in the Cotton Collection.

D = Dr John Davies of Mallwyd; *particularly*, his Dictionarium Duplex.

DDG = Ifor Williams, Detholion o Gywyddau Dafydd ab Gwilym.

Engl.Clyw. = The Englynion y Clyweit (ed. Ifor Williams, Bull. III, p.4).

Ex. Gn. = The Anglo-Saxon Gnomic poem in the Exeter Book.

Hendre G = J. Morris Jones and T. H. Parry-Williams, Llawysgrif Hendregadredd.

HGC = Henry Lewis, Hen Gerddi Crefyddol.

IW = Professor Ifor Williams.

JGE = J. Gwenogvryn Evans.

JMJ = Sir John Morris-Jones.

Laws = A. W. Wade-Evans, Welsh Mediaeval Law.

Le Gonidec = Le Gonidec and de la Villemarqué, Dictionnaire Breton-Français.

LLJ = Professor J. Lloyd Jones, Geirfa Barddoniaeth Gynnar Gymraeg.

LIST OF ABBREVIATIONS

Loth, MG = J. Loth, La Métrique Galloise.

MA = The Myvyrian Archaeology of Wales, 2nd edition (references by page, column, and line).

Mod.W. = Modern Welsh.

M.W. = Mediaeval Welsh.

O.W. = Old Welsh.

Pen. 17 prov. = The proverbs in the Peniarth 17 MS. (ed. H. Lewis, Bull. IV, p.I).

PK = Ifor Williams, Pedeir Keinc y Mabinogi.

Pughe = W. O. Pughe, A Dictionary of the Welsh Language.

RB.Brut = J. Rhys and J. G. Evans, The Text of the Bruts from the Red Book of Hergest.

RBH = The Red Book of Hergest (references to J. G. Evans' edition of the Poetry, by column and line).

RC = Revue Celtique.

Recherches = Th. Chotzen, Recherches sur la Poésie de Dafydd ab Gwilym.

S, see WS.

SE = D. Silvan Evans, Dictionary of the Welsh Language.

Strachan Introd. = J. Strachan, Introduction to Mediaeval Welsh.

Troude = A. E. Troude, Dictionnaire Français et Celto-Breton.

VVB = J. Loth, Vocabulaire Vieux Breton.

WBM = The White Book Mabinogion (references to J. G. Evans' edition, by column and line).

WB prov. = The proverbs in the White Book of Rhydderch (ed. Phillimore, Cymmrodor, VII, p. 138).

Welsh Bard = G. Davies, The Welsh Bard and the Poetry of External Nature, Transactions of the Honourable Cymmrodorion Society, 1912–13.

WG = Sir John Morris-Jones, A Welsh Grammar.

WOP = William Owen (Pughe).

WS or S = William Salesbury; *particularly*, his Dictionary in Englyshe and Welshe.

Yst. Carl. Mag. = S. Williams, Ystoria de Carolo Magno.

ZCP = Zeitschrift für Celtische Philologie.

INTRODUCTION

§ 1

THE POEMS edited in this book form a large section of what has come to be called the "early Welsh nature-poetry". For the most part they are clearly not nature-poems at all as we understand the term, but descriptions of nature do occur mingled with the sententious verse which is their real substance; and this confusion has been explained[1] as the result of a true nature-poetry, corrupted and disintegrated with time, having been used by later sententious poets as a setting for their interpolated and irrelevant maxims. I prefer to regard the descriptive element, which is the smaller, as the irrelevant one, and to treat the poems as essentially sententious or "gnomic" verse, using the term generally applied to this kind of poetry. A *gnome* is a sententious statement about universals, whether about the affairs of men ("human-gnome") or about external nature ("nature-gnome"); it need not be, and usually is not, a current popular saying with an implied moral, as the proverb is, and it need contain no advice or exhortation like the precept. For example, "The vegetable garden is green",[2] that is, "It is the characteristic of vegetable gardens to be green", is a nature-gnome; but "A rolling stone gathers no moss" is a popular proverb whose whole point is in the metaphor and im-

[1] See Glyn Davies, *The Welsh Bard and the Poetry of External Nature*, Cymmrodorion Transactions, 1912–13.
[2] Poem VII.16.i.

INTRODUCTION

plied moral; and "Look before you leap" is an exhortatory precept.

These general gnomic statements may seem to us
unnecessarily obvious, but they were evidently not
thought so at one time, to judge by the gnomic poetry
which is found in other early literatures,[1] particularly
in Anglo-Saxon, where it is very similar to the Welsh.
Bera sceal on haeðe,[2] "a bear is to be found in the
woods", and *Widgongel wif word gespringeð*,[3] "a gadding woman gives rise to comment", from the Anglo-
Saxon gnomic poems, are really very like our "Usual
is the nest of an eagle in the top of an oak"[4] and
"A bad woman causes frequent scandals"[5]; they are all
the outcome of a primitive desire for classification.

For the purposes of these poems it is necessary to
distinguish the nature-gnome relating to universals
from the descriptive statement about nature relating to
particulars ("nature-description"), such as "Mountain
snow, white are the house-roofs",[6] which is a descriptive statement about a particular winter's day. It is this
second type which is the intrusive element, the "nature-
poetry" proper, but it must not be confused with the
true nature-gnomes which are as inseparably part of the
gnomic poetry as the human-gnomes. There are then
two kinds of nature-poetry to be considered, the gnomic
and the descriptive; those poems where the references
to nature are all or almost all gnomes are referred to
here simply as "gnomic", but those where they are

[1] See H. M. and N. K. Chadwick, *The Growth of Literature*,
vol. I, chap. XII.
[2] Cotton Gnomes 29.   [3] Exeter Gnomes 65.
[4] IV.7.i.   [5] VII.16.iii.   [6] III.35.i.

(2)

largely descriptive, together with the usual human-gnomes and a few nature-gnomes, I call "quasi-gnomic". It will be seen that poems nos. III and V are quasi-gnomic; nos. VI, VII, VIII, IX, and the first eight stanzas of IV, are purely gnomic; II is a mixture of gnomic and quasi-gnomic and other stanzas; and the parts of no. I given here are almost all pure nature-descriptions. It is beside the purpose of the present book, which is concerned only with the texts, to deal with the origin and past history of the descriptive nature-poetry and of the gnomic-poetry, or to show how the confusion of the two came about, or what kind of people composed these forms of literature; this would need a separate work if it is to be treated adequately.[1]

The poem no. I is a sketch of a winter's day near the sea shore, and has been included, though it contains few gnomes, because its fine nature-descriptions must be studied in relation to those of the quasi-gnomic poems. The human-gnomes begin to get more frequent in the third lines of the stanzas as the poem proceeds; they are perhaps not "irrelevant" gnomes of the same kind as in the *Eiry Mynydd* stanzas of no. III, for it is at least possible that they are the débris of a dialogue on cowardice;[2] on the other hand they may be no more joined to any story than the *glaɓ allan* verses of no. II with their similar subject, and the whole may be a reminiscence of elegy and saga and gnomes about cowardice, as that poem is. Some of the phrasing is certainly connected in one way or another with the

---

[1] I hope to publish shortly a study of these and other poems, both Welsh and Irish, in which these problems will be examined.
[2] See Ifor Williams, CLH, p.176.

gnomic and quasi-gnomic poetry, for example, *crin caun, crin calaw, cev ewur, hir nos, llum ros, cul hit, kirchid carv crum tal cum clid, briuhid tal glan gan garn carv culgrum cam, bir dit*, and so on; stanza 8 occurs in the Red Book of Hergest, col.1035, ll.13–14, and stanza 22 belongs perhaps to a *Kalan Gaeaf* series like poem V, or is at least influenced by it. Yet it does not read like a mere medley, and is in any case the work of a very competent poet. The last part of the poem in the Black Book belongs to the cycle of Llywarch Hen, and is omitted here because it seems to have no connection with the nature-poetry; it is edited and discussed by Ifor Williams, *Canu Llywarch Hen*.

§ 2

All but two of our poems are found in early manuscripts. No. I is from the Black Book of Carmarthen,[1] now in the National Library of Wales, which was written at the end of the twelfth century. Nos. III–VII are in two manuscripts now in the Bodleian Library, Oxford— the Red Book of Hergest,[2] written at the end of the fourteenth century, and Jesus College MS. 3,[3] written in the first half of the fifteenth century. These poems in Jesus 3 are not copied from the Red Book, but the two are closely related and must have a common not distant manuscript original; perhaps both were copied from the lost parts of the White Book of Rhydderch,[4] which contained a number of the early Red Book poems. No. II is from the Red Book only. No other independent

---

[1] Abbreviated BBC. [2] Abbreviated RBH.
[3] Abbreviated J. [4] See stemma, p.11.

manuscripts of the above poems are known to me, but there are many late copies of them, some at first hand and others more distant; they have no value for the editor and are ignored in the present texts. No. VIII is known only in late transcripts, the earliest of which belongs to the late fifteenth century; no. IX is found in a large number of manuscripts dating from the mid-sixteenth century and later.[1]

Nos. II, IV, V, VI, and three stanzas of VIII amalgamated with VII, were printed from late transcripts by William Owen Pughe in 1792,[2] and in the Myvyrian Archaeology of Wales in 1801,[3] but the first edition (with translations) of nos. I–VII from the BBC and RBH themselves was that of Skene in 1868;[4] he did not use Jesus 3 and gave no variants, and his text is made useless by its misreadings and misprints, to say nothing of the translations. Diplomatic editions of the poems in the BBC and RBH were published by Gwenogvryn Evans in 1907 and 1911 respectively,[5] but there has been no critical edition with translation and notes since Skene's. No. VIII has never been published complete before. No. IX was printed by Rhys Jones in his *Gorchestion Beirdd Cymry* (1773), and in the

[1] On these MSS. see pp.9 ff. and 12 ff.

[2] *The Heroic Elegies of Llywarç Hen.* The "variants" that he gives are mere emendations or the results of scribal errors in late MSS.; for example, many which he gives as from the Red Book show that he was using late and inferior copies.

[3] Pughe's texts were used together with variants from "OLPP", a moderately accurate copy of the Red Book.

[4] *The Four Ancient Books of Wales.*

[5] Vols. 5 and 11 of his Series of Old Welsh Texts.

Myvyrian Archaeology.[1] It was translated by Stephens, *The Literature of the Kymry*, pp.298 ff.

§ 3

Most of the poems have been attributed at one time or another to Llywarch Hen, the sixth-century Welsh prince and reputed author of much early poetry. No. 1 does in fact seem to belong to the Llywarch Hen cycle, but the rest show no internal evidence whatever to connect them with him, and the belief probably arose from certain similarities of style explicable on other grounds,[2] and, as Professor Williams notes,[3] from the position of nos. II–VII in the Red Book immediately before the elegies in the same metre where Llywarch appears. Some late sources make the author the person called Mab Claf ab Llywarch, Macclaf ab Llywarch, Mab Cloch ab Llywarch, or Y Maer Glas ab Llywarch, presumably regarded as a son of Llywarch Hen, though Pughe thought he lived at the end of the fourteenth century.[4] No doubt he is an entirely fictitious character, and Pughe's suggestion is a good one, that the name was invented out of a misunderstanding of some words in the poem RBH, cols.1034–5, *oed mack6y mabklaf*; however, he was evidently looked on as a substitute for Llywarch, an author suitable for writings which the scribe had not evidence or impudence enough to ascribe to Llywarch himself. In fact it is not known who composed the poems.

[1] 21*a*.   [2] See p.3, note 1.
[3] Proceedings of the British Academy, vol. XVIII, p.14, note 1.
[4] *Op. cit.* Introduction.

They cannot be as old as the sixth century in any case, at least in anything like their present form. It is outside the scope of this study to ask how old Welsh gnomic poetry and the more immediate models of these poems may be,[1] but as we have them their language is considerably later than that of the ninth-century Llywarch Hen elegies edited by Professor Williams,[2] which in spite of extensive scribal modernisation preserve many early forms found nowhere in our poems. The latest possible date of composition is fixed by the manuscripts themselves at about 1200 for no. 1 and about 1400 for nos. II–VII. All seven are composed in early types of the englyn metre probably in common use from the ninth to twelfth centuries, though they may have originated much earlier; they lingered on at least down to the fifteenth century as a survival, but were already out of fashion for original composition by the thirteenth.[3] The group nos. II–VII may be dated towards the end of this period, perhaps early twelfth century: the scribe of the Red Book was copying earlier manuscripts, for the readings of v.3.ii, vi.24.ii, and vii.11.ii, indicate an exemplar that used *u* for *w*, and *cyfuaruydant* in iii.2.iii was copied from a text using *uu* or *w* for *f*.[4] Non-mutations of consonants are found in *gocled* (iv.3.i), *bac6ya6c* (iii.20.ii, vi.12.ii), and *brong6ala* (vi.1.iii). All these suggest manuscripts of the late twelfth or early thirteenth centuries. The linguistic evidence is not as helpful as it might be, because in the nature of the poems verbs, valuable date criteria,

---

[1] I hope to show later that gnomic poetry of this kind goes back to the ninth century at least.   [2] CLH.
[3] Cf. RC, xxi, p.33.   [4] But see Cymmrodor xxviii, p.131.

are uncommon; but the following early forms are to be noted: the rare present indicative 3rd sg. in *-id* and *-yd* in frequent use, not only in gnomes but freely as a verb-form for general purposes; passives in *-awr*;[1] *namwyn* occasionally for later *namyn*; *no(c)* for *na*;[1] *llyv6r* for *llwvyr* proved by the rhyme in II.9 and elsewhere; *ny* relative leniting (*ny gara6r*, VI.32.iii); final *-aw(-)* always rhymed in *-aw(-)* and not in *-o(-)*; sporadic "Irish" rhyme (in VI.8 and VII.10 and 11), which Professor Williams believes to be not later than the twelfth century at latest. Further, a group of verses evidently taken from some poem of exactly the same type as no. VI are found on the bottom margin of folio XLII of the Black Book, and the second of them is clearly the same stanza as V.6 and VI.31, with very slight differences (see note to V.6); which shows that this kind of poetry and perhaps these very poems were current already in the twelfth century. On the other hand, if the language is not later than the twelfth century it hardly justifies a date much earlier, for the rarity of "Irish" rhyme and the occurrence of the borrowed Norman French word *menestyr* in rhyme in VI.17.i make it probable that they are later than the Norman Conquest. Stanzas 1–3 and 5 of no. IV are a longer form of the englyn (englyn unodl union) which Professor Loth dates not earlier than the second half of the twelfth century,[2] but it is significant that in stanza 1 the rule about unsymmetrical rhyme in the last couplet is not observed, and that in this *gna6t g6ynt* series stanza 4 is *not* an englyn unodl union but a penfyr;

---

[1] Cf. Loth, *Les Mabinogion*, I, p.28.
[2] RC, XXI, p.37.

so that these verses are scarcely likely to be much later than the mid-twelfth century. Poem II is said by Lloyd (*History of Powys Fadog*, pp.141–2) to have been composed by one Llywelyn Llogell Rhyson, parson of Marchwyail in Powys, "in the ancient style of poetry when the great Eisteddfod was held there in the time of King Edward III"; his source is the spurious "Iolo MSS.", and the statement is obviously an invention based on the occurrence of the word *marchwyeil* as a common noun four times in the poem.

On the dating of no. VIII, which also belongs to this period, see p.11. No. I is certainly older than nos. II–VII. Many rare words and forms, including the use of "*rhy* of possibility", "Irish" rhyme, the frequent *-id* 3rd sg. termination in all kinds of sentences, and the *-int* 3rd pl. present termination, st.8.ii, together with the fact that the poem belongs in some way to the cycle of Llywarch Hen, suggest a comparatively early date, perhaps tenth or early eleventh century.

§4

Nos. VII and VIII are known as the *Bidiau* (called here Bidiau I and II), because of the frequent occurrence of the verb-form *bid*. The two are closely related to each other, but cannot be treated merely as scribal variations of one poem, for the differences are too great and must be due partly to oral transmission; hence they have to be used with caution as sources for emendations of each other.

Bidiau I is in by far the oldest MSS.; the basic text is in RBH, and it is also found in Jesus 3. Bidiau II is in Peniarth MS. 102, pp. 5–6, written by Robert Vaughan (1592–1666) and headed "allan o hen lyfr ar femrwn"; in British Museum Additional MS. 14873, p.189, written by Wm. Morris in 1739; and in Panton MS. 14, f.131, written by Evan Evans (mid-eighteenth century). A version is also found in Peniarth 27.ii, p.89, written in the last quarter of the fifteenth century perhaps by Guttyn Owain,[1] and is thus a much earlier MS. than any of the others; but the text is somewhat different, showing some oral and scribal variation from the other versions and omitting stanzas 8, 9, 10, 12, 13 and 14 (its ninth stanza is the same as Bidiau 1.16) and adding at the end the following verses which do not belong to the Bidiau series:

> O chlywy chwedyl bid hydaw dy vryd;
> ysgafn gwaith gwarandaw;
> ys gwayth ail govyn arnaw.
>
> Na vydd var-vynych, na chwenych gyfrdan;
> na ogan yny bych;
> kadw dy bwyll, twyll na chwenych.

The second is stanza 10 of the version of "Kyssul Adaon" in Llanstephan MS. 27 (see Bull. II, p.121), but is not in the BBC version. Though Peniarth 27 is so much older the text is not so good as that in Peniarth 102, and some of the forms are later; hence I make Peniarth 102 the basis of our text. Some of the gnomes from both Bidiau poems are quoted in the list of proverbs in Peniarth 17[2] (c. 1250), which is thus a very valuable source of early variants.

[1] See J. G. Evans, *Reports on MSS. in the Welsh Language.*
[2] Ed. H. Lewis, Bull. IV, p.1.

The family tree of the Bidiau seems to be this (cf. p.63):

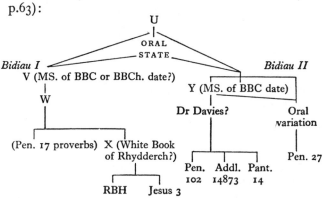

BM. Addl. 14873 is not a copy of Peniarth 102, for it preserves the earlier spelling *ei* for *ai* and has other forms which could not have been taken from Peniarth 102; Panton 14 is on the whole closer to Peniarth 102, but independent of either; the three are all close to each other. The scribal errors common to all, particularly *iad* for *rac* in stanza 1, show that they have one MS. source, perhaps a copy of Dr Davies' (see p. 12). On V, W, and X see the table on p.63.

Though all but one of the MSS. of Bidiau II are very late, and the exception not early, it is evident that like Bidiau I this is an early poem; indications of early date are *no* for *na*, the rare word *eddain* trisyllabic and rhymed in *-in*, "Irish" rhyme in stanzas 8 and 9, *u* for *w* and possibly *i* for *y* in the hypothetical MS. Y, which suggests the late twelfth century, final *t* for final *d* in *lwyt*, and final *c* for final *g* in *bagloc*, etc. in Peniarth 27. The Addl. 14873 copy ends in Welsh with the words:

"Notice the difference between these and those in the Red Book and other old manuscripts, and understand that this poem is very, very old, since there is so much variation between the old copies; apart from the authority of Dr Davies himself." Panton 14 has the same note, with the last phrase expressed "these are the words of Dr Davies". This shows that Bidiau II was known to Dr Davies and believed by him to be very old; also that Addl. 14873 and Panton 14 were copying one of his books. No doubt Peniarth 102 is from the same source.

More than one of the late copies of Bidiau II were known to William Owen Pughe and used by him for variants for Bidiau I. The Myvyrian Archaeology follows him exactly with the addition of variants from "LLPP"[1] for the verses in Bidiau I. Neither used Peniarth 27.

§ 5

The so-called Englynion y Misoedd, "The verses of the months", are twelve stanzas of (normally) eight lines of seven syllables rhyming together. They treat of the twelve months of the year, and consist of an aggregate of unconnected gnomes, the first few generally about the nature of the month concerned and the rest human-gnomes of the usual kind, with a tendency to a religious tone.

There are twelve MSS. known to me. *Llanstephan* 117, *p*.84, by Jeuan ap William about 1545, is the earliest, but it is a carelessly written and not propor-

---

[1] See p.5, note 3.

tionately valuable text. *Peniarth* 99, *p*.547, by Wm. Salesbury (so JGE, Reports), lacks the last three verses where the page has been cut out. *Peniarth* 65, *p*.190, written by Owen John in the late sixteenth century, is a bad and careless version. *BM. Addl.* 14885, *f*.97, also late sixteenth century, is very much damaged round the edges and considerable parts of the lines are lost. *Wrexham* 1, *p*.267, written by John Brooke of Mucklewicke in 1590, is an excellent text, with least misspellings or careless writing or corrupt readings. *Peniarth* 111, *p*.103, written by John Jones about 1610. *Cwrt Mawr* 6, *p*.84, written by Richard the Scribe in 1692. *BM. Addl.* 14873, *p*.80, written by Wm. Morris in 1739, with variants from the " Llyfr Hir ". *BM. Addl.* 14878, *f*.35, written by T. ap Ivan in 1692. *Panton* 18, *f*.59, by Evan Evans in 1769. *Panton* 1, *f*.285, by the same, in 1775. *Panton* 33, *p*.107.[1]

The poem is attributed to Aneirin or Aneirin Gwawdrydd by four MSS. (Addl. 14873, Peniarth 111, at the end, Cwrt Mawr 6, and Panton 33), the first adding that it was about A.D. 510, the other three that it was "in the court of Maelgwn of Gwynedd, king of the Britons". Llanstephan 117 attributes it to Merddin Gwowdrudd (the epithet seems properly to belong to Aneirin); and Peniarth 111 at the beginning, Addl. 14878 (but a marginal gloss adds "others say Aneurin Gwawdrydd composed it"), and a note at the end of the Addl. 14873 version, to Mab Cloch or Mab Claf ab Llywarch (see p.6). Wrexham 1, and Panton 18 and 1, attribute it to Syppyn Cyfeiliog. The first two

---

[1] See J. G. Evans, *Reports on MSS. in the Welsh Language*, II, p.841.

attributions imply that the scribe responsible was completely ignorant of the real authorship and thought it to be of the highest antiquity (and this was believed in Gruffydd Hiraethog's time, early sixteenth century, according to the note in Panton 1). The ascription to Syppyn Cyfeiliog (late fourteenth century) on the other hand points to the belief that it was fairly recent. In the late sixteenth century Sion Tudur wrote a "Digrifwawd neu ymgynhebygiad i Owdl y Misoedd" (in Addl. 14885 and 14873) which makes it likely that the poem had been current for some time before, as he is evidently adapting and parodying a well-established tradition. Lastly, the note that appears in several MSS., that Guttyn Owain (last part of the fifteenth century) wrote three verses to replace three lost from the original poem, shows they were thought to have been current for some time before the middle of the fifteenth century. A posterior date is definitely fixed at 1545 by the earliest MS., Llanstephan 117.

Something can be gathered from internal evidence. There are a number of rare words, some quoted from this source alone by D in his dictionary, some of which were evidently unknown to the seventeenth-century scribes, such as *marianedd*, *molwynoc*, etc.; final -*af* and -*a* are rhymed together, as in *modryda* : *morfa*, which is not early; and final -*aw*(-) with final -*o*(-), as *eos* : *rhos*, which is certainly not earlier than the fourteenth century. On the whole, the middle or later part of the fifteenth century seems a fairly likely date for the composition of the poem in its present form.

Sion Tudur's parody hinted that the Englynion y

Misoedd had already become a widespread popular poem, and this is made certain by the fact that there are at least three versions or recensions to be considered. The first, that given in the text and called here A, is found in all the extant MSS. except Llanstephan 117, and in the *Gorchestion Beirdd Cymry*, where it is attributed to Aneirin Gwawdrydd with no mention of Guttyn Owain. The second version, called here B, is the same as A for the first eight verses, but gives four completely different verses for the last four, which it declares to be the original work of Aneirin or Merddin as the case may be; and adds the four which came last in A with a note that as the original last four were lost, these were composed by Guttyn Owain to complete the mutilated poem. This is found in Llanstephan 117, the earliest MS., and in the MA with a note that the last four were lost since they were not written down, and that when Guttyn Owain had filled the gap, the original four were found in Deheubarth in the "Llyfr Gwyrdd".[1] The MA text uses the *Gorchestion* with variants as from the "Llyfr Hir" for the first eight stanzas, and for the last four gives the B text as from the "Llyfr Gwyrdd", with the A version in footnote. And, though Addl. 14873 gives the A version, it evidently knew B, for it gives a note on f.82, "see the Englynion of the last four months on p.188, which it is thought are the genuine englynion that Aneurin composed; and that it was Guttyn Owain who composed these here to fill the place of the four others which had become quite lost through long space of time"; and on f.188 is the note given by MA (not stating that the

[1] This note is given in Panton 1 as the words of Gruffydd Hiraethog.

source was Llyfr Gwyrdd however) followed by the four englynion in question; these were known to Dr Davies as a note of his is quoted in the margin. The scribe, Evan Evans, clearly followed an A version but tried to combine it with a B one (source Dr Davies?). Two MSS. which give the A version, namely Peniarth 111 and Panton 33, continue with the first verse of the last four in B, without explanation or mention of Guttyn Owain, as if they knew of the existence of a variant September stanza but thought it also due to Merddin or Aneirin respectively. Almost all the MSS. give the A version, including Wrexham 1, which is here taken as the basis for the text, and for the purpose of this edition I follow A; but it must be noted that the earliest MS. gives B, and the belief was known to other scribes. Still there is evidently considerable MS. authority for neglecting the ascription to Guttyn Owain; the source is perhaps some one MS. transcribed by him or associated with his name.

The third version, C, is clearly due to very considerable oral variation, so much as to be almost a new poem; I know of no MS. where it is extant as such, complete, but copious variants are quoted from it in Addl. 14873 from the "Llyfr Hir Nyffryn" and in the MA from the "Llyfr Hir". The last four verses of C are variants on the A version, not on B.

It is not possible to construct a complete stemma for these twelve MSS., as there is much conflation of texts, due probably ultimately to the popular nature of the poem; however, it is noticeable that Llanstephan 117 and Peniarth 99 tend to agree, as do Peniarth 111 and

Cwrt Mawr 6, and Panton 1 and 18 are clearly derived from a text close to Wrexham 1. In editing I have ignored the five latest MSS., which do not contain variants of any value not represented in the rest, and Peniarth 65 which is a poor text; and have used the first six good MSS., namely Llanstephan 117, Peniarth 99, Addl. 14885, Wrexham 1, Peniarth 111, and Cwrt Mawr 6, with Wrexham 1 as basic text, since it is the best early version and only forty-five years later than the earliest. Insignificant orthographical variations and mistakes are ignored.

In editing I make use of the usual signs. One or more letters enclosed in square brackets are my own restorations in the text, thus *man[n]a6c* (VI.20.iii); a blank between square brackets means that something is lost which I have not attempted to restore; one or more letters in pointed brackets are to be deleted, thus *myn⟨yn⟩yd* (III.21.i); one or more letters in italics are an expanded contraction, as ton*n*. The abbreviations of the MSS. of Bidiau II and the Englynion y Misoedd are explained in the notes to those poems.

NOTE. Since writing § 5 Professor T. H. Parry-Williams' remarks on the poem in his *Canu Rhydd Cynnar* (Cardiff 1932; pp.244–5) and his edition, with Sion Tudur's parody, from Peniarth MS. 206, have come to my notice. He mentions fifteen more MSS.; the earliest, Cardiff 5, p.263, which gives fragments only, was written in 1527. Almost all have the A version, the rest B. Apparently he would be willing to accept a fifteenth century date for the Englynion ("Os gwir y cofnod i Gutyn Owain...gyfansoddi pedwar o rai newydd...gallent fod mor hen â'r 15g.").

I

1. Llym awel, llum brin, anhaut caffael clid;
   llicrid rid, reuhid llin,
   ryseiw gur ar vn conin.

2. Ton tra thon toid tu tir;
   goruchel guaetev rac bron ban[n]ev bre;
   breit allan orseuir.

3. Oer lle lluch rac brythuch gaeaw,
   crin caun, calaw truch,
   kedic awel, coed [1]im bluch.

4. Oer guely pisscaud yg kisscaud iaen;
   cul hit, caun barywhaud;
   birr diuedit, guit gvyrhaud.

5. Ottid eiry, guin y cnes;
   nid a kedwir oe neges;
   oer llinnev, eu llyu heb tes.

6. Ottid eiry, guin aren;
   segur yscuid ar iscuit hen;
   ryuaur guint, reuhid dien.

7. Ottid eiry ar warthaw reo;
   gosgupid g[u]int blaen guit tev;
   kadir yscuid ar yscuit glev.

8. Ottid eiry, tohid istrad;
   diuryssint vy keduir y cad,
   mi nid aw, anaw nim gad.

9. Ottid eiry o dv riv;
   karcharaur goruit, cul biv;
   nid annuyd hawdit hetiv.

[1] MS. inibluch.

10. Ottid eiry, guin goror mynit,
    llum guit llog ar mor;
    meccid llvwyr llauer kyghor.

11. Eurtirn am cirn, cirn am cluir;
    oer llyri⟨c⟩[1], lluchedic auir,
    bir diwedit, blaen gvit gvir.

12. Gvenin i gogaur, guan gaur adar,
    dit diulith [   ],
    kassulwin[2] kewin brin, coch gwaur.

13. Guenin i godo, oer agdo rid,
    reuid rev pan vo;
    ir nep goleith lleith dyppo.

14. Guenin ig keithiv, gwirtliv mor,
    crin calaw, caled riv,
    oer divlit yr eluit hetiv.

15. Guenin ig clidur rac gulybur gaeaw;
    glas cimleit[3], cev ewur;
    dricweuet llyvrder ar gur.

16. Hir nos, llum ros, lluid riv,
    glas glan, guilan in emriv,
    garv mir; glau a uit hetiv.

17. Sich guint, gulip hint, kiuuetlauc[4] diffrint,   f. XLVI
    oer callet, cul hit,
    llyw in awon; hinon uit.

18. Driccin i mynit, avonit i gniw,
    gulichid lliw llaur trewit;
    neud gueilgi gueled ir eluit.

---

[1] c *added above the line by a later hand.*
[2] MS. kyssulwin.   [3] MS. cunlleit.
[4] MS. kinuetlauc.

19. Nid vid iscolheic, nid vid e leic unben,
    nyth eluir in dit reid;
    och, Gindilic, na buost gureic.

20. Kirchid carv crum tal cum clid,
    briuhid ia, brooet llum;
    rydieigc glev o lauer trum.

21. Bronureith breith bron,
    breith bron bronureith;
    briuhid tal glan gan garn carv culgrum cam;
    goruchel awel guaetvann,
    breit guir orseuir allan.

22. Kalan gaeaw, gurim gordugor blaen gruc,
    goreuynauc ton mor,
    bir dit; deruhid ych kighor.

23. O kiscaud yscuid ac aral goruit
    a guir deur diarchar,

f.XLVIb.
    tec nos y | ffissccau escar.

24. Kinteic guint, creilum coed,
    crin caun, caru iscun;
    Pelis enuir, pa tir hun?

            .   .   .   .   .

f. XLVII,   35. Gwir i grid, rid rewittor,
    l.8   oeruelauc tonn, brith bron mor;
                Re[e]n rothid duvin kighor.

            .   .   .   .   .

                    II

RBH, col.   1. Bagla6c bydin, bag6y onn,
1032, l.5   hwyeit yn llynn, graenwynn tonn;
                trech no chant kyssul callon.

                    (20)

2. Hir nos, gordyar morua;
   gna6t teruysc yg kymanua;
   ny chytuyd diryeit a da.

3. Hir nos, gordyar mynyd;
   gochwiban g6ynt y6ch blaen g6yd;
   ni th6yll drycanyan detwyd.

4. Marchwyeil bed6 briclas
   a dynn uyn troet o wanas;
   nac adef dy rin y was.

5. Marchwyeil der6 my6n ll6yn
   a dynn vynn troet o gadwyn;
   nac adef rin y uorwyn.

6. Marchwyeil der6 deilyar
   a dynn vyn troet o garchar;
   nac adef rin y lauar.

7. Marchwyeil dryssi a m6yar erni;
   a m6yalch ar y nyth
   a chelwyda6c ny theu vyth.

8. Gla6 allann, g6lychyt redyn,
   g6ynn gro mor, goror ewynn;
   tec a gann6yli p6yll y dyn.

9. Gla6 allan y gan glyd6r,
   melyn eithyn, crin eu6r;
   Du6 reen, py bereist lyv6r?

10. Gla6 allan, g6lychyt vyg g6allt;
    c6ynuanus gwann, diff6ys allt,
    g6el6gan g6eilgi, heli hallt.

11. Gla6 allan, g6lychyt eigya6n,
    gochwiban g6ynt y6ch blaen ca6n;
    g6ed6 pob camp heb y da6n.

III

1. Eiry mynyd, g6ynn pob tu;
   kynneuin[1] bran a chanu;
   ny da6 da o drachyscu.

2. Eiry mynyd, g6ynn keunant,
   rac ruthur g6ynt g6yd g6yrant[2];
   llawer deu a ymgara*n*t
   a phyth ny chyfaruydant[3].

3. Eiry mynyd, g6ynt ae ta6l;
   llydan lloergan, glas taua6l[4];
   odit dyn dirieit diha6l.

4. Eiry mynyd, hyd escut;
   gna6t ym Prydein gynrein drut;
   reit oed deall y alltut[5].

5. Eiry mynyd, hyd ar des,
   h6yeit yn llynn, g6ynn aches;
   h6yr hen, ha6d y ordiwes.

6. Eiry mynyd, hyd ar dro;
   chwerdyt[6] bryt 6rth a garo;
   kyt dywetter 6rthyf chwedyl
   mi a atwen veuyl lle y bo[7].

7. Eiry mynyd; graennwyn gro;
   pysc yn ryt; clyt y ogo;
   kas vyd a oreilytto.

8. Eiry mynyd, hyd ar daraf;
   gna6t gan gynran eiryan araf,
   ac ysgynnu o du corof[8]
   a disgynnu bar ar araf.

---

[1] J, kenevin.
[2] RB, g6yryant *with second* y *cancelled*; J, g6yryant.
[3] *sic* J; RB, chyfuaruydant.
[4] J, tana6l.   [5] J, alldut.   [6] J, chwerdit.
[7] J, mi atwen veuyl lle bo.   [8] J, o tu corff.

(22)

9. Eiry mynyd, hyd kyngr6n;
   llawer a dywedeis[1], os g6nn;
   anhebic y[2] hafdyd h6nn.

10. Eiry mynyd, hyd hella6t[3];
    gochwiban g6ynt y6ch barga6t t6r;
    tr6m, a 6r, y6 pecha6t.

11. Eiry mynyd, hyd ar neit;
    gochwiban g6ynt y6ch g6enbleit uchel;
    gna6t ta6el yn deleit.

12. Eiry mynyd, hyd ym bro;
    gochwiban g6ynt y6ch blaen to;
    nyt ymgel dr6c yn lle y bo.

13. Eiry mynyd, hyd ar draeth;
    collyt[4] hen y uabolaeth;
    drycdrem a wna dyn yn gaeth.

14. Eiry mynyd, hyd yn ll6yn,
    purdu bran, buan jyrchwyn;
    iach ryd, ryueda6t[5] pa g6yn[6].

15. Eiry mynyd, hyd my6n br6yn,
    oer micned; med y gherwyn[7];
    gna6t gan bob anauus g6yn.

16. Eiry mynyd, brith bronn t6r,
    kyrchyt[8] aniueil glyd6r;
    g6ae wreic a gaffo drycwr.

17. Eiry mynyd, brith bronn kreic,
    krin kalaf, alaf dichleic;
    g6ae 6r a gaffo drycwreic.

---

[1] J, dyweis.
[2] J, *om.*
[3] J, ella6t.
[4] J, collit.
[5] *sic* J; RB, ryuedot.
[6] J, ae k6yn.
[7] J, yng6erthr6yn.
[8] J, kyrchit.

18. Eiry mynyd, hyd yn ffos,
    kysgyt[1] g6enyn yn didos;
    kytuyt lleidyr a hir nos.

19. Eiry mynyd; kynglhennyd [yn] auon;
    h6yrweda6c yng kynnyd[2]
    ny moch dieil meuyl meryd.

20. Eiry mynyd, pysc yn llynn;
    balch heba6c, bac6ya6c unbynn;
    [3]nyt ef a geiff pa6b a uynn[3].

col.1029
21. Eiry myn⟨yn⟩yd; coch blaen pyr;
    llidia6c lluossa6c[4] | ongyr;
    och, rac hiraeth vy mrodyr!

22. Eiry mynyd; buan bleid,
    ystlys diffeith6ch a dreid;
    gna6t pob anaf ar dieid[5].

23. Eiry mynyd, hyd nyt h6yr;
    dyg6ydyt[6] gla6 o awyr;
    megyt[7] tristit lleturyt llwyr.

24. Eiry mynyd; eilion[8] ffraeth;
    gowlychyt[9] tonneu glann traeth;
    keluyd kelet y aruaeth.

25. Eyry mynyd, hyd my6n glynn;
    g6astat uyd haf, araf llynn;
    baryfl6yt re6; gle6 y erchwynn.

---

[1] J, kysgit. RB *has ll.2 and 3 transposed, with marks of transposition.* J *has them transposed without the marks.*

[2] J, yngklynnyd.   [3-3] *See note.*

[4] J, lluoessauc.   [5] J, direid.

[6] J, dyg6ydit.   [7] J, megit.

[8] J, eilyon.   [9] J, gowlychit.

26. Eiry mynyd; brith bronn g6yd;
kadarn vy mreich a'm ysg6yd,
eidunaf na b6yf gannml6yd.

27. Eiry mynyd, ll6mm blaen ca6n,
cr6m blaen g6rysc, pysc yn eigya6n;
lle ny bo dysc ny byd da6n.

28. Eiry mynyd, pysc yn ryt,
kyrchyt[1] car6 culgr6m cwm[2] clyt;
hiraeth am uar6 ny weryt.

29. [3]Eiry mynyd, hyd yg koet;
ny cherda detwyd ar troet;
meckyt[4] ll6uyr llawer adoet.

30. Eiry·mynyd, hyd ym bronn;
gochwiban g6ynt y6ch blaen onn;
trydyd troet y hen y ffon.

31. Eiry mynyd, hyd ar na6,
hwyeit yn llynn, g6yn*n* ala6;
diryeit ny mynn g6aranda6.

32. Eiry mynyd; coch traet ieir;
bas d6fyr myn yt leueir;
chwenneckyt meuyl ma6reir.

33. Eiry mynyd, hyd esgut;
odit a'm dida6r o'r byt;
rybud y dr6ch ny weryt.

34. Eiry mynyd, g6ynn y gnu[5];
ys odida6c wyneb ku o gar
gyt a mynych athreidu.

[1] J, kyrchit.   [2] J, cum.
[3] J *transposes st.*29 *and* 30.   [4] J, meckit.   [5] J, y gu.

35. Eyry my[ny]d, g6ynn to tei;
bei traethei daua6t a wypei geuda6t
ny bydei gymyda6c[1] neb rei.

36. Eiry mynyd, dyd a doeth[2];
bit glaf[3] pop tr6m; ll6m lletnoeth;
gna6t pob anaf ar a[n]noeth.

IV

RBH,
col.1031

1. Gna6t g6ynt o'r deheu; gna6t atneu[4] yn llann;
gna6t g6r g6ann godeneu;
gna6t y dyn ofyn chwedleu;
gna6t y vab ar uaeth uoetheu.

2. Gna6t g6ynt o'r d6yrein; gna6t dyn bronrein balch;
gna6t m6yalch ym plith drein;
gna6t rac traha tralleuein;
gna6t yg gwic kael kic o urein.

3. Gna6t g6ynt o'r gocled[5]; gna6t rianed[6] chwec;
gna6t g6r tec yg G6yned;
gna6t y deyrn arl6y g6led[7];
gna6t g6edy llynn lleturyded.

4. Gna6t g6ynt o'r mor; gna6t dygyuor llan6;
gna6t y uan6 uagu hor;
gna6t y uoch turya6 kylor.

5. Gna6t g6ynt o'r mynyd; gna6t meryd y mro;
gna6t kael to yg gweunyd[8];
gna6t ar laeth maeth dyn creuyd;
gna6t deil a g6yeil a g6yd.

---

[1] J, ganmoda6c.   [2] *sic* J; RB, ac dooeth.
[3] J, glas.   [4] J, adneu.
[5] *sic* RB; J, gogled. [6] J, rianet.
[7] J, g6yled.   [8] J, yngg6yned

6. [1]Gna6t o vastardaeth[2] grynn6ryaeth ar wyr,
   a g6raged dr6c meduaeth,
   a chyni ar wyr a gor6yr waethwaeth.

7. Gna6t nyth eryr ym blaen dar,
   ac yg kyfyrdy g6yr llauar;
   gol6c vynut ar a gar.

8. Gna6t dyd ac anll6yth yg kynnlleith gayaf[3];
   kynreinyon kynr6ytieith;
   gna6t aelwyt diffyd yn diffeith.

9. Crin calaf a llif[4] yn nant;
   kyfnewit Seis ac aryant;
   digu eneit mam geublant.

10. Y deilen [honn] a dreuyt[5] g6ynt,
    g6ae hi oe thynget;
    hen hi, eleni y ganet.

11. Kyt boet bychan, ys keluyd
    ⟨yd⟩[6] adeil adar yg gor6yd coet;
    kyuoet vyd da a detwyd.

12. Oerwlyb mynyd, oerlas ia;
    ymdiryet y Du6 nyth d6ylla;
    nyt edeu hirbwyll hirbla.

V

1. Kalan gaeaf, kalet gra6n,   RBH, col.
   deil ar gych6yn, llynnwynn lla6n;   1031, 30
   y bore gynn noe vynet
   gwae a ymdiret y estra6n.

---

[1] *Stanza from* J; *see note*, p.52.   [2] J, JGE, bastardaeth.
[3] J, gayat.   [4] J, lif.
[5] J, dry6yt.   [6] *See note*, p.52.

2. Kalan gayaf, kein gyfrin,
   kyfret awel a dryckin;
   g6eith keluyd y6 kelu rin.

3. Kalan gayaf, cul hydot,
   melyn blaen bed6[1], g6ed6 hauot;
   g6ae a haed meuyl yr bychot.

4. Kalan gayaf, cr6m blaen g6rysc;
   gna6t o benn dirieit teruysc;
   lle ny bo da6n ny byd dysc.

5. Kalan gaeaf, gar6 hin,
   anhebic y gynteuin;
   namwyn Du6 nyt oes dewin.

6. Kalan gaeaf, kein gyfreu[2] adar,
   byrr dyd, ban cogeu;
   trugar daffar[3] Du6 goreu.

7. Kalan gayaf; kalet cras;
   purdu bran, buan ovras[4];
   am g6ymp hen chwerdit g6en g6as.

col.1032 8. Kalan gaeaf, cul kerwyt;
   gwae wann pan syrr; byrr vyd byt;
   g6ir g6ell hegar6ch[5] no phryt.

9. Kalan gayaf, ll6m godeith,
   aradyr yn rych, ych yg gweith;
   o'r kant odit kedymdeith.

---

[1] *sic* J; RB, bedu.   [2] J, gyffreu.
[3] J, darfar.   [4] J, buan bras.
[5] J, herar6ch.

(28)

VI

1. Gorwyn blaen onn, hirwynnyon vydant
   pan dyuant ym blaen neint;
   brong6ala[1] hiraeth y heint[2].

2. Gorwyn blaen neint; deweint hir;
   kei*n*mygir[3] pob kywreint;
   dyly bun p6yth hun y heint.

3. Gorwyn blaen helic; eilic pysc yn llynn;
   gochwiban g6ynt y6ch blaen[4] g6rysc man;
   trech anyan noc adysc.

4. Gorwyn blaen eithin a chyfrin a doeth,
   ac a[n]noeth disgethrin;
   namyn Du6 nyt oes dewin.

5. Gor6yn blaen meillyon; digallon llyf6r;
   lludedic eidigyon[5];
   gna6t ar eidil oualon.

6. Gorwyn blaen ka6n; g6ythla6n eidic;
   ys odit ae diga6n—
   g6eithret call y6[6] caru yn ia6n.

7. Gorwyn blaen mynyded; rac anhuned gayaf
   [7]crin ka6n; tr6m callwed[7];
   rac ne6yn nyt oes wyled.

8. Gorwyn blaen mynyded; hydyr oeruel gayaf;
   crin ka6n, cr6ybyr ar ued;
   whefris[8] g6all yn alltuded.

RBH, col.1033

---

[1] J, bron*n* waly.   [2] J, y heneint.
[3] J, kein megir.   [4] *om.* J.
[5] *sic* J; RB, edigyon.   [6] *om.* J.
[7-7] *sic* J; RB, crin ca6n tr6m crin ka6n tr6m.
[8] J, chweffris.

(29)

9. Gorwyn blaen der6, chwer6 bric onn,
   rac hwyeit g6esgerit[1] tonn;
   pybyr p6yll; pell oual y'm kallon.

10. Gorwyn blaen der6, chwer6 bric onn;
    ch6ec[2] eu6r, ch6erthinat ton*n*;
    ny chel grud kystud kallon.

11. Gorwyn blaen egroes; nyt moes caledi;
    katwet ba6p y eiryoes;
    g6aethaf anaf y6[3] anuoes.

12. Gorwyn blaen banadyl, kynnadyl[4] y sercha6c,
    goruelyn kangeu bac6ya6c;
    bas ryt; gna6t hyfryt yn huna6c.

13. Gor6yn blae*n* auall; amgall pob dedwyd;
    wheueryd[5] y arall,
    a g6edy karu gadu g6all.

14. Gorwyn blaen auall; amgall pob dedwyd;
    hir dyd; meryd mall;
    cr6ybyr ar wa6r; carchara6r dall.

15. Gor6yn blaen coll geir Digoll bre[6];
    diaele uyd pob ffoll;
    g6eithret cadarn cad6 aruoll.

16. Gor6yn blaen corsyd; gna6t meryd yn dr6m,
    a ieuanc dysgedyd;
    ny thyrr nam6yn ffol y ffyd.

17. Gorwyn blaen elestyr; bit venestyr pob drut;
    geir teulu yn ysg6n,
    gna6t gan aghy6ir eir t6nn.

---

[1] *sic* J; RB, g6esgereit.   [2] *sic* J; RB, chec.
[3] *om.* J.   [4] *om.* J.
[5] J, chweferyd.   [6] J, bro.

18. Gorwyn blaen gruc; gna6t seithuc ar l6fyr[1];
    hydyr vyd d6fyr[2] ar dal glan;
    gna6t gan gywir eir kyvan.

19. Gor6yn blaen br6yn; kym6yn bi6[3];
    redega6c vyn deigyr hedi6;
    amgeled[4] a*m* dyn nyt ydi6.

20. Gor6yn blaen redyn; melyn kada6arth;
    mor vyd diwarth[5] deillon;
    redega6c man[n]a6c meibon.

21. Gor6yn blae*n* kyra6al; gna6t goual ar hen,
    a g6enyn yn ynyal;
    namyn Du6 nyt oes dial.

22. Gorwyn blaen dar; didar drychin;
    g6enyn yn uchel; geuvel crin;
    gna6t gan rewyd rych6erthin.

23. Gor6yn blaen kelli, gogyhyt y g6yd,   col.1034
    a deil deri dyg6ydyt[6];
    a wyl a gar, g6ynn y uyt.

24. [7]Gorwyn blaen der6; oeruer6 d6fyr;
    kyrchit bi6 blaen bet6er6[8];
    g6nelit aeth saeth y syber6.

25. [9]Gorwyn blaen kelyn, kalet [angawr],
    ac ereill eur-agoret;
    pan gysco pa6b ar gylchet
    ny ch6sc Du6 pan ryd g6aret.

---

[1] J, lyf6r.   [2] J, d6f6r.
[3] J, lli6.   [4] *sic* J; RB, amgeled amgeled.
[5] J, diwall.   [6] J, dyg6ydyd.
[7] J, *om. st.*24–7.   [8] RB, betuer6.
[9] RB, gor6yn blaen kelyn kalet ac ereill eur agoret.

26. Gorwyn blaen helic; hydyr elwic gorwyd;
hirdyd deilyedic;
a garo y gilyd nys dirmic.

27. Gorwyn blaen br6yn, briga6c vyd
pan danner dan obennyd;
med6l sercha6c syber6 vyd.

28. Gorwyn blaen yspydat; hydyr hwylyat gorwyd;
gna6t sercha6c erlynnyat;
g6nelit da diwyt gennat.

29. Gor6yn blaen ber6r; bydina6r[1] gorwyd;
kein gyfreu[2] coet y la6r;
ch6erdyt[3] bryt 6rth a gara6r[4].

30. Gorwyn blaen perth; hywerth gorwyd;
ys da p6yll gyt a nerth;
g6nelyt agheluydyt[5] annerth.

31. Gorwyn blaen perthi; kein gyfreu adar[6],
hir[6] dyd, da6n goleu;
trugar daffar Du6 goreu.

32. Gorwyn blaen erwein[7] ac elein yn ll6yn;
g6ychyr g6ynt, g6yd migyein[8];
eirya6l ny gara6r[9] ny gyghein.

33. Gorwyn blaen ysga6; hydyr ana6 unic;
gna6t y dreissic dreissya6;
g6ae a d6c daffar o la6.

---

[1] J, bydina6d.
[2] J, geffreu.
[3] J ch6erdit.
[4] J, anghara6r.
[5] J, angheluydyd.
[6] J, a drahir.
[7] J, erpein.
[8] J, nugyein.
[9] sic J; RB, gara6l.

VII (BIDIAU I)

1. Bit goch crib keilya6c, bit annyana6l y lef
   o wely buduga6l;
   llewenyd dyn, Du6 ae ma6l.

RBH,
col.1030

2. Bit la6en meichyeit 6rth ucheneit g6ynt;
   bit ta6el yn deleit[1];
   bit gna6t afl6yd ar diryeit.

3. Bit guhudyat keissyat; bit gynifiat[2] g6yd;
   a bit gynnwys[3] dillat;
   a garo[4] bard bit hard rodyat.

4. Bit[5] le6 unbenn a bit avwy,
   a bit vleid ar ad6y;
   ny cheid6 y wyneb ar ny rodwy.

5. Bit vuan redeint[6] yn ardal mynyd;
   bit yn gheuda6t[7] oual;
   bit anniweir annwadal.

6. Bit aml6c marcha6c, bit ogela6c lleidyr;
   t6yllyt g6reic goluda6c;
   kyueillt bleid bugeil dia6c.

7. [8]Bit aml6c marcha6c[8]; bit redega6c gor6yd;
   bit uab llen yn ch6anna6c[9];
   bit anniweir deueirya6c.

8. Bit gr6m bi6 a bit l6yt bleid;
   esgut gor6yd y ar heid;
   g6esgyt g6a6n gra6n yn y wreid.

---

[1] J, *om. the line.*   [2] RB, gnifiat; J, gnifyat; P, A, gynifiad.
[3] J, gyn6ys.   [4] J, gara.
[5] RB, bit avwy unbenn a bit le6; P, A, bid lew unben a bid
awy vryd; J, bit le6 unbenn a bit avwy vleid ar ad6y.
[6] J, redec.   [7] J, angheuda6t.
[8-8] *om.* J.   [9] J, bit chwanna6c mab llen.

9. Bit gr6m bydar, bit tr6m keu;
   esgut gorwyd yg kadeu;
   ¹g6esgyt g6a6n gra6n yn y adneu¹.

10. Bit haha bydar; bit annwadal ehut;
    bit ynuyt ymladgar;
    detwyd yr² ae g6yl ae kar.

11. Bit d6fyn³ llynn; bit lym⁴ g6aewa6r;
    bit gwarant le6⁵ gle6 6rth a6r;
    bit doeth detwyd, Du6 ae ma6l⁶.

12. Bit euein alltut; bit disgythrin drut;
    bit chwanna6c ynvyt y chwerthin;
    ⁷bit l6m ros, bit tost kenin⁷.

13. Bit wlyb rych; bit uynych mach;
    bit g6yn claf, bit la6en iach;
    bit ch6yrnyat col6yn, bit wenwyn gwrach.

14. Bit diaspat aele⟨u⟩; bit aë bydin;
    bit basgadur⁸ dyre;
    bit drut gle6 a bit re6 bre.

15. Bit wenn g6ylan⁹, bit vann¹⁰ tonn;
    bit hyuagyl g6yar ar onn;
    bit l6yt re6; bit le6 callonn.

1-1 om. J.
   ² sic P, and PP 223; A, ir; RB, J, or.
   ³ P, A, dwfn; RB, dyf6n; J, d6fyr.
   ⁴ sic J; P, A, llym; RB, lynn.
   ⁵ P, A, gwarandeu glau; PP 121, warancleu glew; RB, granclef gle6; J, grangklef gle6.
   ⁶ P, A, nawdd; RB, J, ma6r.
   7-7 sic J; RB, om.; P, A, bid lwm rhos bid cost cennin.
   ⁸ RB, J, besgittor.
   ⁹ sic J; RB, g6ylyan.   ¹⁰ J, wann.

16. Bit las lluarth[1]; bit diwarth eirchyat;
    bit reinyat y ghyuarth[2];
    bit wreic dr6c ae mynych warth.

17. Bit grauanga6c[3] iar; bit trydar gan le6;
    [4]bit ynvyt ymladgar[4];
    bit tonn callon gan alar.

18. Bit wynn t6r; bit orun[5] seirch;
    bit hoffder lla6er ae heirch;
    bit l6th chwanna6c, bit ry[gy]nga6c cleirch[6].

VIII (BIDIAU II)

1. Bid gogor[7] gan iar; bid trydar[8] gan lew,
   bid ofal ar a'i car[9];
   bid tonn calon rac galar[10].

   Peniarth
   102, f.5

2. Bid aha byddar; bid anwadal ehud;
   dirieid[11] bid ymgeingar,
   dedwydd yr[12] a'i gwyl a'i car.

3. Bid gywir baglawg;[13] bid rygyngawd gorwydd;
   bid fab llen yn chwannawg;
   bid anniwair deueiriawg[14].

---

[1] J, buarth; P 2, lle fuarth.   [2] J, ynghyuarch; *see note*, p. 65.
[3] J, grauaug.   [4-4] *om.* J.
[5] RB, J, or6n.   [6] J, ringa6c cleiryach.
[7] P 2, graviad; A, P, gogor.
[8] A, trygar; P 2, dridar; Pt 14, trydar.
[9] P 2, ofnad ar a gar; A, bid ofal ar ei car.
[10] P, iad calar; A, iad galar; P 2, rrac galar; RB, gan alar; Pt 14,
iad galar *with* gan alar *written above.*
[11] *sic* A; P, P 2, diriaid.   [12] P 2, ar; A, ir.
[13] A, gwir baglawl; P 2, gywir bagloc; Pt 14, gywir baglawg.
[14] *sic* Pt 14; A, P, daueiriawg; P 2, dau eiriawc.

4. Bid amlwg marchawg; bid ogelawg lleidr;
   twyllid gwraig goludawg[1];
   cyfaillt blaidd bugail diawg.

5. Bid gwyrdd[2] gweilgi; bid[3] gorawen[4] tonn;
   bid cwyn pob galarus,
   bid aflawen hen heinus.

6. Bid wlyb rhych; bid fynych mach[5];
   bid chwyrn[6] colwyn, bid wenwyn[7] gwrach;
   bid cwynfan[8] claf, bid lawen iach.

7. Bid chwyrniad colwyn, bid[9] wenwyn[10] neidr;
   bid nofiaw[11] rhyd wrth beleidr;
   nid gwell yr odwr[12] no'r[13] lleidr.

8. Bid anhygar diriaid, bid ffer pob eweint[14];
   bid heneint[15] i dlodedd;
   bid addfwyn yn ancwyn medd.

9. Bid dwfn llynn; bid llym gwaywawr[16];
   bid gwarant lew[17] glew wrth awr;
   bid doeth dedwydd, Duw a'i nawdd.

10. Bid llawen meichiaid[18], gwynt a gyfyd;
    [19]bid dedwydd ar ei naid[19],
    gnawd aflwydd ar ddiriaid.

---

[1] A, oludawg.
[2] P 2, gwerdd.
[3] A, bod.
[4] P 2, gorwen.
[5] *So* P 2; A, P, fach.
[6] P 2, chwyrniad.
[7] P 2, wenwynic.
[8] P 2, kwynus.
[9] A, beid.
[10] P 2, wenwynic.
[11] P 2, noviad.
[12] *sic* P 2; A, odtwr; P, otdwr.
[13] A, na'r.
[14] *sic* A; P, Pt 14, ewaint.
[15] *sic* A; P, henaint.
[16] *sic* A; P, gwauwawr.
[17] A, P, gwarandeu glau; *see* RBH, v.11.ii *note.*
[18] *sic* P, Pt 14; A, meichiad.
[19-19] P, A, ar ei naid bid dedwydd; *see note,* p. 66.

11. Bid gyhuddgar[1] ceisiad; bid[2] gynifiad gwydd;
    bid gynnwys gan[3] dillad;
    bid garu bardd gan roddiad.

12. Bid wenn gwylan, bid fann tonn,
    bid hyfagl gwyar ar onn,
    bid lwyt rew[4], bid lew calon.

13. Bid lew unben a bid awy vryd,
    a bid lleiniad yn ardwy[5];
    ni cheidw ei wyneb ni roddwy.

14. Bid llymm eithin, a bid eddain alltut[6];
    chwannawg drut[7] i chwerthin;
    bid lwm rhos, bid tost[8] cennin.

IX (ENGLYNION Y MISOEDD)

1. Mis Jonawr[9], myglyd dyffryn,
   blin trulliad[10], trallawd[11] klerddyn,
   kul bran, anaml llais gwenyn,
   gwac buches, diwres odyn;
   gwael gwr anwiw[12] i ofyn;
   gwae a garo[13] i dri gelyn;
   gwir[14] a ddyvod[15] Kynvelyn[16]
   "gorev kannwyll pwyll i ddyn."

---

[1] P, []yḍdgar; A, guhuddgar; P 2, kyhuddgar.
[2] A, byd.   [3] P 2, dyn.
[4] A, P, Pt 14, lwytrew.   [5] A, yr.
[6] P, alldud; A, alltut; PP 115, alldut.
[7] sic A and Pt 14; P, drud.   [8] sic J; P, A, cost.
[9] sic P 99, P 111, C; W, LL, A, ionor.
[10] sic P 99, P 111, C; W, trulliaid; LL, trilliad; A, trylliad.
[11] A, treigl[ad].   [12] A, anwyl.
[13] LL, A, gar.
[14] sic LL, P 99, A, P 111, C; W, gwyr.
[15] A, ddowod.   [16] LL, kyvelin.

2. Mis Chwefrol[1], anaml[2] ankwyn[3],
 llafurus pal ac olwyn;
 knawd gwarth o fynych gysswyn[4];
 gwae heb[5] raid a wnel achwyn;
 tri ffeth a dry dryg-wenwyn[6],
 [7]kyngor gwraic, murn[8], a chynllwyn;
 pen ki[9] ar vore wanwyn;
 gwae a laddodd[10] i vorwyn;
 [11]diwedd dydd da fydd i fwyn[11].

3. Mis Mawrth, mawr rhyfic[12] adar,
 chwerw[13] oerwynt ar ben talar[14];
 hwy vydd hindda[15] no heiniar[16];
 hwy pery llid no galar[17];
 pob byw arynaig[18] esgar;
 pob edn[19] a edwyn i gymar;
 pob peth a ddaw drwy'r ddaiar
 ond y marw, mawr i garchar.

4. Mis Ebrill, wybraidd gorthir,
 lluddedig ychen, llwm tir,
 gwael[20] hydd, gwareus clusthir[21];
 knawd osb[22] er nas gwahoddir;

[1] P 99, A, chwefror. [2] LL, anvall; A, annyall.
[3] P 111, amkwyn; C, amgwyn.
[4] LL, gynllyn; C, gynllwyn. [5] P 99, pob.
[6] LL, a vag drwc; P 99, a vac dryc; A, a dry yn ddrwg; C, P 111, a dry drwc. [7] LL, kyngol, gwraic, a mynych gychwyn.
[8] A, myr. [9] LL, kic; P 99, A, cil.
[10] A, laddo. [11-11] om. LL, P 99, A, P 111, C.
[12] LL, rryddig. [13] LL, amyl.
[14] sic LL, P 111, C; P 99, A, ar dalar; W, ar ben dalar.
[15] A, hinon. [16] LL, hen iar (!). [17] A, nag alar.
[18] sic P 111; W, C, a ryfic i ysgar; A, a raneg i ymyskar; LL, P 99, om. the line.
[19] A, pob dyn. [20] P 111, gwyl; LL, gael.
[21] W, gwareus glusthir; LL, chwrws klustir; P 99, chwareus clusthir; A, char[ ]s klysthir; P 111, gwareus klysthir; C, chwraeys glysd hir. [22] sic A, P 111, C; LL, osber ir; W, P 99, gwest.

aml bai pawb lle nis kerir[1];
gwyn i fyd a vo kowir;
knawd difrawd ar blant enwir[2];
knawd gwedi[3] traha tranck hir.

5. Mis Mai, difrodus[4] geilwad,
klyd pob klawdd i ddigarad[5];
llawen hen diarchenad[6];
hyddail koed, hyfryd anllad[7];
hawdd kymod lle bo kariad;
llafar koc a bytheiad;
nid hwyrach[8] mynd i'r farchnad
[9]croen yr oen no chroen y ddavad[9].

6. Mis Mehevin, hardd tiredd,
llyfn mor, llawen[10] marianedd,
hirgain dydd[11], heinif[12] gwragedd,
hylawn[13] praidd[14], hyffordd mignedd[15];

[1] P 99, LL, ni cherir.
[2] *sic* P 99, A, P 111, C; W, anwir; LL, aniwir.
[3] *sic* LL, W, C; A, P 111, wedi; P 99, wedy.
[4] LL, diwrydes.
[5] C, ddigariad.
[6] LL, a di archenad; C, ddiarchenaid; P 99 *transposes ll.3 and 4*;
C *and* P 111 *give the first six lines in the order* 1-2-3-6-4-5; LL
gives 1-3-2-6-4-5.
[7] A, amkad.
[8] *sic* P 111; W, mynd yr; LL, A, yr a i'r; P 99, vyd i'r; C, gyn
ebrwydd yn y.
[9-9] *sic* P 99, LL (groen), P 111, A (na), C (a); W, groen yr oen
no'r hen ddavad.
[10] *sic* P 111, C; LL, llawen meranedd; W, llawn marianedd;
P 99, llawen myranedd; A, llawen mirianedd.
[11] *sic* A; W, LL, P 99, P 111, C, ddydd.
[12] *sic* P 111; C, W, LL, P 99, A, heini.
[13] LL, hylawnt.
[14] A, brig; W, pridd.
[15] LL, mugynedd.

Duw a gar[1] pob tangnevedd[2],
Diawl a bair pob kynddrygedd[3];
pawb a chwennych anrrydedd;
pob kadarn gwan i ddiwedd.

7. Mis Gorffennaf, hyglyd[4] gwair,
   taer tes, toddedig kessair[5];
   ni char gwilliad[6] hir gyngrair[7];
   ni lwydd hil korff[8] anniwair;
   llwyr dielid mefl mowrair[9];
   llawn ydlan[10], lledwag kronffair;
   gwir a ddyvod[11] mab maeth Mair,
   "Duw a farn, dyn a levair".

8. Mis Awst, molwynoc[12] morva,
   llon gwenyn, llawn[13] modryda;
   gwell gwaith kryman no bwa;
   amlach das no chwarwyva[14];
   ni lafur ni weddia,
   nid[15] teilwng iddo i fara;
   gwir a ddyfod[16] Sain[17] Brenda
   "nid llai kyrchir[18] drwc no'r da".

[1] sic LL, P iii, C; W, P 99, A, bair.
[2] sic A; LL, W, P 99, P iii, C, tyngnefedd.
[3] C, gynddaredd; A, kyngryddeg; P 99, transposes ll.5 and 6.
[4] C, myglyd.   [5] A, kesail; C, geisair.   [6] A, P iii, C, gwilliaid.
[7] sic LL, A, P iii, C; W, gyngair; P 99, gyggrair.
[8] P 99, P iii, C, o gorff.
[9] LL, dielid dirmic mevyl vowrair; A, dielir melf mowlair;
C, ddiliad mel. LL and C transpose ll.5 and 6.
[10] P 99, llwm ydlan; W, LL, P iii, C, llwm ydlam; A, llawn
hyd lan.   [11] A, ddowod.
[12] LL, moel wynoc; P 99, C, malwenoc; A, molwenog; P iii,
malwynawg altered to molwenog.
[13] P iii, llawen; A, llon gwenwyn llawn bodryda.
[14] sic W, P iii; P 99, chwerwyfa; A, chwryddfa; C, chwaryddfa;
LL, amlach das o hyd no chwarwyva.
[15] W, ni; LL, ni bydd.   [16] A, ddowod.   [17] A, C, saint.
[18] LL, P 99, drwc no da; P iii, C, gyrchir y drwg na'r da;
A, drwg na'r da.

9. Mis Medi, mydr[1] ynGhanon,
   aeddfed oed[2] yd ac aeron;
   gwae[3] gan hiraeth fy nghalon;
   golwg Duw ar dylodion[4];
   gwaetha gwir[5] gwarthrudd[6] dynion;
   [7]gwaetha da drwy anudon[7];
   [8]traha a threisio[9] gwirion[10]
   a ddiva yr etifeddion[11].

10. Mis Hydref, hydraul[12] echel,
    chwareus hydd, chwyrn awel;
    knawd ysbeilwyr[13] yn rryfel;
    knawd lledrad[14] yn ddiymgel;
    gwae ddiriaid[15] ni[16] ddawr pa wnel;
    trychni ni hawdd[17] i ochel;
    [18]angau i bawb sy ddiogel,
    amau fydd y dydd y del.

---

[1] *sic* LL, P 111, C; W, mudyr; A, mydr amkanon; P 99, mytr.
[2] C, oedd; A, coed.
[3] *sic* C, P 111; W, gwayw; LL, gwaiw; P 99, gwaew; A, gwyf.
[4] A, dyledion.
[5] P 99, da.
[6] LL, gwarth dynion; A, gwarthae; P 111, gwartha gwirion *altered from* gwarthrudd dynion; C, gwerthu'r gwirion.
[7-7] P 99, *om.*
[8] LL, gwaeth a thrin a dreisio dynion.
[9] P 99, threisu'r.
[10] C, gwyrion; A *illegible.*
[11] *sic* P 111, C; LL, gwaetha diva diva'r ydiveddion; W, ytifedd-ion; P 99, a ddiva'r plant a'r wyrion; A *illegible.*
[12] W, A, hydrawl.
[13] LL, C, ysbeilwynt; A, ysbeilwr; P 111, ysbeilwynt mewn *altered to* ysbeilwyr yn.
[14] P 111, lladron; A, lladrad.
[15] LL, dduried ni ddawr beth anel; A, dyn ni ddawr pa nel.
[16] C, ni ddaw.
[17] LL, P 111, C, nid rrwydd.
[18] A, [   ] a ddaw yn ddiogel.

11. Mis Tachwedd, tuchan[1] merydd,
    bras llydnod, llednoeth koydydd;
    awr a ddaw drwy lawenydd[2],
    awr drist drosti a dderfydd;
    y da nid eiddo'r[3] kybydd[4],
    yr hael ai rhoddo pieifydd[5];
    dyn a da'r byd a dderfydd,
    da nefol tragwyddol fydd.

12. Mis Rhagfyr[6], byrddydd, hirnos,
    [7]brain yn egin, brwyn yn rhos,
    tawel gwenyn ac eos;
    [8]trin yn niwedd kyfeddnos;
    adail dedwydd yn ddiddos;
    adwyth diriaid heb achos;
    yr hoydl er hyd i haros
    a dderfydd yn nydd[9] a nos.

---

[1] A, P 111, C, tychan.
[2] sic C; P 111, llawenydd; LL, W, lywenydd; A, llywenydd.
[3] W, eidd r; LL, eio y.   [4] ll.5–7, om. A.
[5] W, ai rhydd ai pieifydd; LL, ai rroddo bievydd; P 111, ai rroddo pievydd; C, ai rhoddo biau'r bydd.
[6] W, rhacfyr.
[7] C, brain yr y egin brwyn yn y rhos; A, ar egin.
[8] sic A; W, P 111, C, ynghyfedd ddiweddnos; LL, yngyvedd nos.
[9] A, ag yn nos; C, a gyn nos; LL, yn nydd yn nos.

(42)

NOTES

I

Sт.1. Metre, cf. JMJ, Cerdd Dafod, p.313; but see Loth, MG, II.1, p.236.

l.i. **caffael** is probably to be read *caffel*, as often, to give rhyme with *awel*.

l.ii. **llicrid**, i.e. is flooded. *Llygru*="to corrupt, spoil, mar"; see PK, p.171.

l.iii. **ry** of possibility, see Strachan Introd. p.60, i.e. the grass, etc. is frozen so hard that one could stand on a stalk without breaking it.

Sт.2. Englyn byrr crwcca.

l.ii. **guaetev**, "outcries" (of the wind), cf. *goruchel awel guaetvann*, st.21, l.iv.

l.iii. "Scarcely can one stand up outside." **Orseuir**, cf. v.7.ii, note. With this line cf. st.21, l.iv.

Sт.3, l.i. **lluch**, "a lake", occurs in place-names, as *Ll6ch E6in, Ll6ch Ta6y*, WBM, 503. Borrowed from Irish *loch*. The phrasing of *lle lluch* is unusual; leg. *lly*, fr. *lly⁺* in *gwely*, "bed", as in st.4? Or tr. "cold is the place; there is dust (reading *lluch=lluwch*) blown before the tumult of winter"?

Brythuch, cf. *taryan y mrythwch*, BT, p.11, 6–7; *bum gawr ym mrythwch*, ibid. p.48, 20; *brydeu anaraf brythwch gaeaf*, MA, 189a, 43; *brythwch=ymlad*, D. Here="tumult". Cf. the two meanings of *gawr*.

l.iii. **kedic**, cf. *llit kedic, lla6 dreissic dra6s*, RBH, 1240, 19. On this passage Loth (ACL, I, p.409) says "'le vent bataille'; je suppose que *kedic* est un dérivé de *cad*"; but cf. the *cad* in the common place-name *cadnant*="noisy stream"? Not all the Cadnants can be sites of battles; cf. also Afon Cedig running into Lake Vyrnwy. **Coed im bluch**; the dash over the second *i* is quite distinct in the MS., but the emendation is necessary for metre and improves the sense. **Bluch** is a crux. *Blwch*="box", but that cannot be the meaning here. Is it Breton *blouch*, "sans poil, sans barbe, nu, découvert" (Troude)? (cf. *Bluchbard* in Nennius="beardless" or "shaven bard"?); or cf. Irish *blog*, "a fragment"?

Sт.4, ll.ii and iii. **barywhaud...gvyrhaud**, "bearded...bowed", adjectival termination; see Loth, ACL, I, p.407, and WG, p.396.

Sт.5, l.1. **eiry**; a second *eiry* has been partially erased in the MS.

(43)

Note that the *-y* in these instances is sometimes syllabic, as in Mod.W. *eira*, and sometimes not, as normally in M.W. See WG, p.177. **Cnes**, cf. CLH, p.177; it must mean "surface" here.

l.ii. **oe**="to their", cf. CLH, p.177.

Sᴛ.6, l.i. **aren** for *arien*, a S. Welsh form; cf. PK, p.278.

l.iii. **dien**, "grass", cf. *g6aet ar dien*, BT, p.33, 9; *attpaur a dien* BBC, f.xᴠɪɪɪ.12. Cf. Bull. ᴠɪ, p.213, but H. Lewis, HGC, p.283.

Sᴛ.7, l.i. **reo**; *o* for *w* is an old spelling occurring in the oldest parts of the BA.

l.ii. **gosgupid**, a ἅπαξ λεγόμενον, but clearly fr. *go* + *(y)sgub*— = "sweeps".

Sᴛ.8. Cf. RBH, 1035, 13–14. L.ii, see CLH, p.177.

Sᴛ.9, l.i. **o dv**, cf. *o'r tu allan*="on the outside".

l.iii. **annuyd**, cf. LLJ, s.v. *annwyt* 2.

Sᴛ.10, l.ii. "Bare are the timbers of the ship at sea." Or, with a comma at *guit*, "bare are the trees, the ship is at sea"; the first of these gnomes is quite natural but the second is not, for a ship at sea is more characteristic of summer than winter in primitive seafaring. The picture is of a ship with its sails taken in before the winter storm.

Sᴛ.11, l.i. **eurtirn**, pl. of *eurddwrn*; cf. *cledyf eurd6rn*, WBM, 455, "gold hilted sword". *Claideb órduirn*="mit goldenem Griff", Windisch, s.v. *órduirn*. Perhaps "handles" here? For evidence that early Welsh (blowing) horns had gold rims, see RBH, 1037, 19, where *arwest*="rim". Cf. the Anglo-Saxon gold-rimmed drinking horns, as the Taplow specimen, see British Museum Guide to Anglo-Saxon Antiquities, p.64.

Cluir. A *cluir* occurs BBC, f.ᴠɪɪɪ.9="chorus", which does not seem to fit here. Can it be plural of *cloer*, "a slit-window or recess", such as are found in castles; and tr. "drinking horns round the window shelves"? i.e. a kind of sideboard (IW). The whole line in any case seems to be a gnomic one.

l.ii. **llyri**, "paths", pl. of *llwrw*.

Auir, note rhyme in *ŵyr*, the older pronunciation.

l.iii. **gvir**, "bent", cf. *gvyrhaud*, st.4, l.iii.

Sᴛ.12, l.i. **gogaur**="fodder", a dialect word in Carmarthenshire. The meaning is here that the bees live in their hive on their stored supplies.

l.ii. Something has fallen out in the MS., and the rhymeword in *-awr* is missing.

Diulith, "bleak", fr. *gwlydd*, "soft". Note *th* for *t*=*dd*.

NOTES

l.iii. **kassulwin**="white-cloaked".

St.13, l.i. **agdo**, LLJ, "cover" (?). Cf. Loth, ACL, I, p.403, "froide est la *surface*? du gué. Il gélera quand il y aura gelée.... *Angdo < ang*, large étendu".

l.iii. **goleith...dyppo**, cf. CLH, p.177.

St.15, l.ii. **cimleit**, cf. *cyflaith*; "*glas gyflaith y llech*, Medd. Mydd., ii.150, cf. 78, 606," SE; "*Elebiarni*, the name of some plant, Medd. Mydd. 284", *ibid*. Loth (ACL, I, p.413) reads *cunlleit* with the MS. and suggests *cynlladd*, "first cut (plants)"? and tr. "verts sont les émondes"; but this is a ghost word.

  Cev ewur, i.e. the cow-parsnip stalk is hollow and withered in winter.

St.16. This and the next verse seem to be meant as weather signs.

l.ii. **emriv** seems to be a ἅπαξ λεγόμενον; compound of *rhiw*? Or read *emliv=ymliw*, "quarrelling"? (IW.)

St.17, l.i. **kiuuetlauc**, i.e. *cywethlog*; cf. *cywaethyl*, RB.Brut, 34 = "argue, quarrel"; *cywaethla*="litigabit", *ibid*.153; *cywethyl*, *ibid*.6. *T* for *th*, as often in O.W. and the BBC.

  Diffrint, "valley" *< dwfr + hynt*="watercourse", perhaps here in its original meaning.

l.ii. **callet**, a pl. of *celli*.

St.18, l.i. *i mynit*, cf. IV.5.i, note.

St.19. This stanza appears to be out of place and to belong to the Llywarch Hen dialogue series; cf. BBC, f.LIVb, 13. It seems Llywarch is reproving Cyndilig for not playing the part of a warrior. See CLH, p.178.

St.20, l.i. Loth, ACL, I, p.433, "recherche le cerf au front courbe une combe abritée". But "au front courbé" would be *talgrum*.

l.iii. **ry** of possibility, cf. st.1, l.iii, note.

St.21. This stanza seems to have been confused with another in a different metre. A couplet *bronureith—bronureith* has been clumsily joined on to an englyn of 10, 7, 7. On the first couplet, Ifor Williams (Beirniad, II, 1912, p.58) notes that this is an old metric technique found in the Gododdin; and Loth, MG, II, p.6, notes the tendency in BT to repeat the rhyme word, as in *popcant id cuitin, id cuitin pop cant*.

l.v. **guir**, see v.8.iii, note.

  Orseuir, see v.7.ii, note.

St.22. This stanza is from a Kalan Gaeaf series, but it looks like a reshuffling of st.10 above. See CLH, p.179.

St.23 belongs to the story of the latter part of the poem, see Introduction, p.4, and CLH, pp.179–80.

Sr.24. See CLH, p.180.

l.iii. The story of the poem; ten stanzas are here omitted as irrelevant.

Sr.36. The last in the poem, omitted as irrelevant.

II

Stanzas 4–6 probably do not belong to the poem, as they seem to be part of a story whose meaning is now unknown; perhaps someone has been betrayed by an indiscreet confidence and imprisoned as a result, but the references to "saplings" are obscure. Possibly the verses got added to the poem on the analogy of *marchwyeil*, "saplings", at the beginning of stanza 7, if that is not itself part of the preceding.

Sr.1, l.i. "Serried is the host, budding is the ash"? There seems to have been a considerable confusion in the Celtic languages between at least three roots[1]: one *bac+-* with meanings "crowd, cluster, curl, sprig, bud, tip"; the second *bacc+-* = "angle, hook"; and the third *bacal+* (Irish), *bacl+* (Welsh) = "staff, crozier, crook", fr. Latin *baculum* (see Thurneysen, *Kelto-Romanisches*, p.39). The confusion of "curl" and "crook" is natural, and it is not always possible to distinguish the roots and meanings. *Meaning* (1), "crowd, cluster, curl, sprig, bud, tip". *Bagad* = "nonnulli, aliquot, turba, turma; utimur pro racemo uvarum", D. *Racemus* = "bagedyn", *ibid*. *Bagadog* = "hung with clusters of grapes or berries". *Gorwyn blaen afall blodau-fagwy*, "of clustering flowers", MA, 143a, 7. *Goruelyn kangeu bagwyawc*, "clustering branches", VI.12.ii. *Ac uch wynep gwin gwineu-vagwy*, "auburn curls", MA, 158b, 44. *Bagwy* = "blaer" (leg. "blaen"), Arch. Brit. 214a. Breton *bagad* = "troupe", Troude. Irish *baclach* = "a crowd", Dinneen; *bachall* = "a curl", *bachallach* = "ringleted", *bachla* = "germ, sprout, or bud", *bachlóg*, "a bud, sprout, twist, curl", *ibid*. *Bachlach* = "curl'd or frilled", Arch. Brit., Irish-English Dict., s.v. *bachlach*. Welsh *baglurun* = "budde", *blagurun* (with metathesis) = "burgen", WS. *Meaning* (2), "staff, crozier, crook, hook, crooked". *Baglog* = "baculatus", D. *Bachall* = "staff, crozier, pilgrim's staff", Meyer, Conts. *Asc6rn y chefyn oed ar weith bagyl*, "her backbone was like a crook", WBM, 166. *Kynn bum kein-vagla6c*, "before I was crook-backed", RBH, 1036, 1. *Baglan brenn*, "wooden crook", *ibid*. 1036, 9. Derivative, "one bearing a crook, a shepherd"; Irish *bachlach*, "a shepherd, rustic, boor, clown", Conts. *Bachlach* =

[1] In Jespersen's sense of "root", see *Progress in Language*, pp.113–15.

"cleric, priest, monk", Conts. *Ni chwennych morwyn vynach baglawg*, MA, 852b, 13 (i.e. "one bearing a crozier"? So Thurneysen, *op. cit.* p.39, on Breton *belek*, "a priest". But cf. *bachall*, "tonsuring, clipping, shearing"; *do gabail bachla*="clericatum suscepit", Conts. What is this *bachall*?). With root *bacc⁺-*, Welsh *bach*, "hook, nook, corner, angle"; *bachog*="hooked". Irish *bac*, "an angular space...a crozier...a hook", Dinneen. Cf. *bacach*, "a cripple", *ibid.*? i.e. "one who goes on crutches"? Or cf. Welsh *cyrfachu*, "to wither"? Note *bach* frequent in place-names, as *Y Fach Wen*, near Llanberis, *Y Fach Ddeiliog*, near Bala; = "nook".

l.ii. **graenwynn**, cf. III.7.i, *graennwyn gro* (cf. *g6ynn gro mor*, st.8, l.ii). It probably stands for *graeanwynn*, cf. *daer, dair*: *daear*, but might be for *granwyn*, "white-cheeked" or "white-bearded", which would be a more natural epithet of a wave, but less natural in III.7. Note also *gran a gro*, RBH, 1035, 33, leg. *graean*. The scribes appear to have felt some difficulty with the word.

ST.2, l.i. See Bull. 1, p.118, where *dyar* is explained by IW as "sad"; "efallai bod dau *ddyar* yn Gymraeg, un yn golygu *twrf* ac yn cyfateb i'r ferf *do-garim* a rydd Windisch, W. 495". For "noisy", cf. *dyar*="sonitus, strepitus, sonare, strepere, hinc gorddyar", D.

ST.3, l.iii. See IV.11.iii, note. Contrast the *diriaid* who is led astray by his own *drycanyan*.

STS. 4, 5 and 6. See p.46 and p.9.

ST.4, l.ii. **gwanas**, see PK, p.200. Here="fastening".

ST.5, l.iii. Cf. "Scél Mucci Mic Dathó" (ed. N. K. Chadwick, *An Early Irish Reader*), p.10, *asbert Crimthand Nia Nair, ni thardda do rún do mnaib*, "said Crimthann Nia Nair, 'do not let out your secret to women'".

ST.6, l.ii. **carchar** can hardly be "prison" here on the analogy of *gwanas* and *cadwyn*. For the meaning "fetters" see PK, p.135.

ST.7, l.i. **erni** shows that *dryssi* is singular here, though usually plural with singular *drysien*. Is it a collective?

ST.9, l.ii. JGE, *eithin*, but the *y* is quite distinct in the MS.

l.iii. **lyv6r**, cf. VVB, p.177, *lobur*, "infirme, faible"; *anhela* gl. *lobur*, *ibid.* Irish *lobur*. If the modern *llwfr* is derived from this *lobur* it must be a later form metathesised from the *lyv6r* which is found here and elsewhere in the early poems. The rhyme shows the form is correct here, as elsewhere.

ST.10, l.ii. **diff6ys**, common in place-names, = "precipice".

ST.11, l.iii. i.e. "achievement without its own proper genuine talent is not enough".

NOTES

III

Sᴛ.1. **eiry mynyd**. *Eiry* is normally monosyllabic, and it is quite
possible that the original form of this common refrain was *eiry
ym mynyd*, "snow on the mountains", which would be a preferable
construction. But dissyllabic *eiry* occurs frequently in e.g. poem 1
(see st.5, note). The usage in the later Eiry Mynydd poems varies;
e.g. MA, 358a, st.1, *Eiry* scanned dissyllabic; st.2, *Eir* but scanned
dissyllabic; st.3, *Eira*.

l.ii. **canu**, cf. *gnawd i farn* (leg. *fran*) *fynych ganu*, MA,
361b, 8, i.e. "to make a noise with its voice". Some literal-minded
person objected that the raven is hardly a song-bird, hence MA,
854a, 25, *nid cynnevin bran a chanu*.

Sᴛ.3, l.i. **taól**, cf. DDG, p.8, 47, *talm sydd iddi os tolia*, and p.116,
arbed neu gynilo yw toli. Or is it < *taflu*, cf. *ysgawn* < *ysgafn*, etc.,
and tr. "The wind tosses it"?

l.ii. **lloergan**, see RC, xlii, p.353, "pleine lune", Loth.

l.iii. "A mischievous man is rarely without litigation."
Dirieit, see iv.11.iii, note.

Sᴛ.5, l.ii. **aches**, cf. LLJ, s.v. *aches*.

Sᴛ.6. Englyn unodl cyrch.

l.ii. **chwerdyt**. Note the spelling in -*yt* (and so often elsewhere; but J always spells -*it*); the rhyme here with *bryt* shows
that the vowel is *y*, not *i* (cf. vi.23, *dygóydyt* rhyming with *uyt*).
See CLH, p.165, s.v. *llewychyt*. This must be a different form of
the 3rd sg. -*id* ending, presumably from -*etī*+, while the other is
from -*ītī*+; see WG, pp.332 and 323. Note that these -*awd*, -*id*,
-*yd* forms *need not* stand at the head of the sentence (contrast WG,
p.332), e.g. v.7.iii, *am góymp hen* chwerdit *góen góas*.

Sᴛ.7, l.i. **graennwyn**, see ii.1.ii, note.

l.ii. **ogo**, note the loss of final *f*. **Y**=*yn*, cf. PK, p.122.

Sᴛ.8. Note the metre; **daraf**, **araf**, and **corof** are monosyllabic
and proest rhyme; the irrational vowel has been assimilated to the
word-vowel in spelling.

l.iv. A gnome about the "chieftain" might be expected,
parallel to l.iii, and it seems to refer to his dismounting. Is *bar-
ar-arf* a phrase descriptive of dismounting? But what is **araf**? It
cannot be *araf*, "slow" ("and for anger to come down upon the
tardy"), because the rhyme shows it is monosyllabic. Is it *arf*,
"a weapon", again? Tr. "and for anger to come upon (i.e. find)
a weapon", and read in line ii *varaf*, "and for a chieftain to have
a fine beard"; or keep *araf* in l.ii and read *varaf* in l.iv, "and for
wrath to come down because of an insult", taking *barf*, "beard",

(48)

the sign of the warrior, to="honour" or "insulted honour", cf. *wyneb*, "face", in the same meanings, and cf. RBH, 1048, 10, *meuyl barueu*?

St.9, l.i. **kyngr6n**, see CLH, p.77. Here="hunched".

l.ii. **os g6nn**, see PK, p.118. "Truly."

St.10. Englyn byrr crwcca.

l.i. **hella6t** < *hela*, ="hunted", cf. *gvirhaud, barwyhaud*, 1.4. The *ll* is due to assimilation either of the *-gh* of the root or the *h* which seems to occur in several cases of this *-awd* termination; see WG, p.396, and Strachan Introd. p.83. Is the *h* on the analogy of the future in *-hawd*? (See Strachan Introd. p.84.)

l.iii. **a 6r**, MS. *a6r*; the metre shows it must be two syllables. Cf. WBM, 474, *Oi, a6r, cany at mor mar6 dl6s ynda6...*, leg. *oi a 6r*, "Good sir", etc.

St.11. Englyn byrr crwcca.

l.iii. *teleid* = *telediw*, D.

St.13, l.ii. **collyt** means more than "loses" here; rather, "feels the loss of".

l.iii. i.e. an ugly face makes a man feel inferior, hampers him.

St.14, l.ii. See v.7.ii, note. Note *j* for consonantal *i*.

l.iii. **ryueda6t**; note *-ot* written for *-awt* in the RB text, a late spelling due to the RB scribe. See WG, p.95.

Pa, "why", see WG, p.290.

St.15, l.ii. **y gherwyn** = *yngh gherwyn*, see iv.5.i, note.

Pob, see note on vi.2.ii.

St.16, l.i. **brith**, i.e. with snow.

St.17, l.ii. **alaf**, see Loth, ACL, i, p.449; and CLH, p.169. Cf. *cyfalaf*, "wealth", and Irish *alamh*, "cattle".

Dichleic, see WBM, 504, where *cleicaw*=to plunge. Does it mean here that the cattle do not enter the water because it is too cold?

l.iii. Cf. RC, xlv, p.8, *mairg gach aon isa frithe drochmná*, "woe to everyone who has got a bad wife".

St.18, l.iii. Cf. Cotton Gnomes, l.42, *þeof sceal gangan þystrum wederum*, "the thief goes in darkness". Note *kytuyt* with the second *t*=*dd*, a sign of copying from a MS. in the earlier spelling.

St.19, l.i. **kynglhennyd**, cf. Wm. Salesbury, *Llysieulyfr* (ed. Stanton Roberts), p.114, *cynglennyd*, "a kind of liverwort". Cf. D, *Botanology, cynghlennydd yr afon*, "y llefanog, llyfiau'r afu, llinwydd yr afon, clust yr assen, lichen, secoraria, hepatica". Hugh Davies, *Welsh Botanology*, " =iungermannia, epiphylla, river star-tip". ACL, I, p.40, *epatica=y geglynnydd*; see N.E.D. s.v. *liver-wort=hepatica*.

l.iii. **kynnyd**=*cynnif*, see Bull. II, p.299. But in Mod.W.= "to progress, gain ground"; therefore, "the slow succeeds"?

ST.20, l.ii. **bac6ya6c**, see II.1.i, note.

l.iii. JGE prints *nyt ef ageiff ageiff pa6b auynn*, but the first *ageiff* is distinctly crossed through, and by the original scribe, in RB. J *nyt ef a geif pa6b a vynn*.

ST.21, l.i. **pyr**, from Latin *pyrum, pyrus, pirum, pirus*, "pear tree"?

l.ii. **ongyr**, "spears", cf. MA, 191a, 52; 211a, 9; 247a, 45; 291b, 48; RBH, 1442, 18, *cledyfeu cochyon cochyn onger*.

ST.22, l.ii. *treiddio*, "penetrate", but cf. BBC, f.xxx.2, *lluid yv vy bleit, nim treit Guendit*, "Gwendydd does not *visit* me".

l.iii. **dieid** cannot be a scribal error for *dirieid* in spite of the reading of J, because the rhyme is in *-dd*. =*diheid*, "wretched" (with loss of *h* after the accent, cf. *deau=dehau*, etc.)? Cf. RBH, 1391, 27–8, *Maon Meiryonnyd, mor diheid a6ch bot heb aruot heb aervleid*, "how sad it is", etc.; *ibid.* 1384, 24–5, *Mor diheid hynny mor dyhir*, "How sad that is, how grievous". Or is it *di+eidd* in *eiddig*, "eager, greedy" (cf. *eidic am gic*, "eager for the flesh", RBH, 1045, 44) and *eiddgar*, "zealous"? Therefore *diaidd=* apathetic?

ST.24, l.i. **eilion**, "deer"; cf. BBC, f.xxxb, 11, *bit itau in aelau, eilon indi*, and RC, XXXVIII, p.52. Cf. *elain*, "a fawn", and Irish *elit*, "a deer".

Ffraeth="parod, cyflym", see IW in Arch. Camb. 83, 356.

l.iii. If we can read *kelyt* it would be preferable to translate "the skilful conceals his design", since the imperative is extremely rare in these gnomes; see st.6, l.ii, note.

ST.25, l.iii. **erchwynn**, "the side of a bed", that is, the edge or outside, away from the wall. The brave man takes his place (in battle, etc.) on the side nearest danger. **Y**=*yn*, cf. PK, p.122.

ST.27, l.iii. See v.4.iii, note.

ST.28, l.ii. The reading of J is interesting as suggesting an exemplar of BBC spelling.

l.iii. **weryt**, <*gwared*, Mod.W.="deliver", but cf. st.33, l.iii, where the meaning "avail" is clear.

ST.29, l.ii. **detwyd**, see IV.11.iii, note.

l.iii. i.e. "swings the lead"? or, "the coward is a cause of much harm"? **Adoet**, see WBM, 472, *Nyd athoed kyweithyd hebda6 eiroet ny wnelei ae anaf ae adoet arnei*; *ibid.* 478, *Yspadaden*

Penka6r, na saethutta ni bellach, na uyn anaf ac adoet a'th uar6 arnat. "Hurt", "harm".

Sᴛ.31, l.i. **na6** : *nofio*, with (regular) loss of *-f* (<*m*) in a monosyllable, cf. *llaw* : *llofrudd*. In the form *nawf -f* is restored by analogy. Cf. Bull. ᴠɪ, p.135.

l.iii. **diryeit**, cf. ɪᴠ.11.iii, note.

Sᴛ.32, l.ii. "Where it babbles."

Sᴛ.33, l.iii. **trwch**, cf. DDG, p.94, l.4, *trwch fum gyfarfod a'r tri*, "unfortunate was I to meet the three". Compare the Irish proverbially unavailing *robad do throich*, "warning to the doomed", *The Vision of MacConglinne* (ed. K. Meyer), p.71.

Sᴛ.34, l.iii. **athreidu**, cf. *treiddio*, st.22, l.ii, note. Ll.ii and iii = "too frequent visiting is ill-received"?

Sᴛ.35. Note the mutations with the 3rd sg. imperfect.

l.ii. **ceuda6t**, cf. BBC, f.ʟɪ.1, *kid y lleinv keudaud nis beirv calon*. "Mind." See LLJ.

Sᴛ.36, l.iii. **annoeth** = "a fool".

IV

Stanzas 9 and 11–12 are of the quasi-gnomic type. Stanza 10 belongs to the poem RBH, col.1036, and has somehow got inserted here. These last four verses have been treated as part of poem ɪɪ by WOP and MA, because they are not *gna6t* stanzas like the rest, but they belong definitely to ɪᴠ in RBH and Jesus 3, and there is no good reason for separating them.

Sᴛ.1. Englyn unodl union, but without cywydd rhyme.

l.i. **gna6t**, "customary", Irish *gnáth*. The meaning of "gnawd XY" is "it is an attribute of X to be Y"; there is no specific implication that X is usually Y but not always.

Atneu, see LLJ, s.v. *atneu*, and cf. *atneu gan berchenna6c*, WB prov. 25, and *atneu kyheryn gan gath*, *ibid*. 26. The idea is that deposits of treasure are made in a church as a safe place, cf. H. Lewis, HGC, p.190, where *Llan adneu* is translated "*Depositi Monasterium*". But note LLJ, *ibid*. (4), *dodi mewn bedd*, which might possibly fit here; and cf. Loth, RC, xʟɪɪ, p.345.

Sᴛ.2. Unodl union.

l.i. **bronrein**, "with a stiff breast". *Rhain* = "stiff", cf. *celaned rain*, "stiff corpses", MA, 143 b, 17; *kynvrein bronrenion*, "haughty chieftains", BBC, f.xxx.12.

l.iv. **gwic**. The ordinary meaning in Mod.W. is "wood", cf. *coedwig*. But see Loth, RC, xʟɪ, pp.390 ff., where he suggests compare Irish *fich*, "battle". "Usual for ravens to get flesh in a battle" would perhaps be more in accord with early ideas.

Sᴛ.3. Unodl union.

l.i. Note non-mutation of *c* in *gocled*, and see p.7.

l.ii. Is this an indication of where the poem was composed? Cf. Ifor Williams, *The Poems of Llywarch Hen* (Proceedings of the British Academy, vol. xviii), p.14.

Sᴛ.4, l.iii. **kylor**, cf. *bunium = clor, cylor*, Hugh Davies, *Welsh Botanology*; *kylor =* "bunium, earthnut", *ibid.* p.178. Irish *ciclamen, malum terrae*, gl. *in cularán*, RC, ix, p.228.

Sᴛ.5. Unodl union.

l.i. **meryd**, "a fool, dullard", cf. *mergidhaam*, gl. *ebesco* (VVB, p.184), and *meryd mall*, vɪ.14.ii, and *gna6t meryd yn dr6m*, vɪ.16.i, and *o'i ferydd benglog*, Gwyneddon, ɪɪɪ, p.27, l.55; Irish *mearaidhe =* "amadán", O'Clery.

Y mro. This method of writing *yn*, with the final nasal assimilated to the following consonant and lost (but *yg* before *g*, *k = yng(h)*), is common in the poems and no doubt represents the pronunciation, a sort of *sandhi*. I leave the MS. spelling throughout to indicate the probable pronunciation and to limit the number of emendations; it is to be understood always as *ym mro*, etc.

Sᴛ.6. Omitted in the late copies, e.g. BM. Addl. 14873, f.164, and in WOP and the MA. It is erased in the RBH and illegible to me (though evidently legible to JGE); Skene notes this and gives a corrupt text in a footnote as from the Book of Llywelyn Offeiriad; but he must have been following a late transcript, as that MS. (i.e. Jesus 3) reads the same as JGE's reading of RBH.

l.i. *o bastardaeth* J, JGE; the *b* is probably a miscopying for *v*.

Crynn6ryaeth, "baseness", "boorishness", cf. Ifor Williams, *Dafydd Nanmor*, p.163.

l.ii. "And for bad women to be feasted on mead."

Sᴛ.7, l. ii. **kyfyrdy**, see Bull. ɪɪ, p.308.

Sᴛ.8, ll.i–ii. A crux. What is **anll6yth**? Leg. *a tanll6yth*, "with a blazing fire", but the non-mutation of *t* would then be difficult to explain. **Kynnlleith**; *Cynllaith* is a district in Powys, which cannot fit here; the word also means "battle", "slaughter", e.g. BBC, f.ʟɪɪɪ.4, which Thurneysen (*Kelto-Romanisches*, s.v.) derives from *lectos⁺*, "death"; but adds that as an adjective it = "flüssig", : *dadleitho*, "to dissolve". Tr. therefore "usual is a blazing fire in the damp of winter"? **Kynr6ytieith** must be a compound of *ieith*, "tongue"; *r6yt = r6yd* with *t* for *d = dd*? If so, "chieftains are free of speech"?

l.iii. Cf. *arfedauc y diffyd diffeith*, Pen. 17 prov. 83, and *dinas y diffyd diffeith, ibid.* 209, and *gna6t aelwyt diffyd yn diffeith*, WB prov. 97.

Sт.9, l.ii. Cf. Giraldus Cambrensis, *Descript. Kamb.* 1, c.8, "They (the Welsh people) pay no attention to commerce", and Chotzen, *Recherches*, p.115, "Quant aux Anglais que Dafydd ab Gwilym a connus personnellement, eux aussi sont intéressés dans le commerce". On this and the following stanzas see p.51.

l.iii. **geublant**, cf. PK, p.143.

Sт.10. This verse is from RBH xi, where it belongs: the differences would be accounted for by oral transmission. I insert **honn** from RBH, 1036, 29 to make a regular penfyr (Loth type 4).

Sт.11. Englyn byrr crwcca.

ll.i–ii. "Though it be small, ingenious is the nest of the birds in the border of the wood."

l.ii. The **yd** is unmetrical and must be a case of dittography, for if **adeil** were a verb, **bychan** and probably **boet** would have to be plural.

Gor6yd; cf. *O Fangor...hyd orwyd Meirionyd meidriad*, MA, 148 b, 1; *Kyfliw eiry gorwynn gorwyt Epynt, ibid.* 158 a, 1; *Teir allawr gwyrthuawr...yssy rwg mor a gorwyt a gwrt lanwed, ibid.* 248 b, 46; *Eiry mynydd gwynn gorwydd, ibid.* 362 a, 12; *hawdd nawdd yn gwasgawd gorwydd, ibid.* 848 b, 52. The meaning seems to be "border" or "slope" or "upland", perhaps originally "upland boundary", cf. the two uses of *ael*="brow" or "border"; and with this passage cf. DDG, p.59, 1, *yn ael coed*. Skene, "tall trees", a guess for this passage; note WOP, "skirt of the wood". Derivation? Rhyme shows the last syllable is *-wŷdd*, not *-ŵydd*.

l.iii. **detwyd**. Mod.W. "happy". The early meaning seems to be "fortunate" in the sense of one who is born under a lucky star, with whom everything prospers, and so "blessed" (cf. A.S. *eadig*, which means either "prosperous" or "blessed"), from which, with slight extension of meaning, sometimes "righteous". Cf. *bet6n dedwyd dianghut*, "If I had been fortunate thou wouldst have escaped", RBH, 1037, 38; cf. CLH, p.71. *Nyt eidun detwyd dyhed* (i.e. it is only the unlucky under-dog that wants a revolution), RBH, 1035, 23; so *dedwyd a gar dadoluch*, Pen. 17 prov. 196 and Engl.Clyw. 45. *Ny cherda detwyd ar droet*, "the prosperous does not journey on foot", iii.29.ii; *ny reit y detwyd namyn y eni*, "the fortunate needs but to be born", WB prov. 172 and Engl.Clyw. 51. *Pa achaws y kyffroassawch vivi eiryoet yar vyg gwastat detwydyt* (Lat. *felicitatem*), RB.Brut, 67. *Pan vych detwyd byd gyfnessaf ytt duhvn; Kystal yw hynny a erchi ytt o bydy gyuoethawc a detwyd* ("wealthy and successful") *bot wrthyt duhvn*, tr. *dapsilis interdum*

(53)

notis et largus amicis Cum fueris, dando semper tibi proximus esto;
Bull. II, p.32. *Guledic deduit*, "blest Lord", BBC, f.xx b, 4. *Adail dedwydd yn ddiddos*, "the house of the fortunate is sound",
Englynion y Misoedd, 12, 5. *Dedwydd* is used in the Welsh Bible
as a translation of μακαρίος, Latin *beatus*, e.g. in the Beatitudes.
But cf. Loth, RC, XXXVI, pp.174–5, "Le sens propre était *sage*, qui
réfléchit et sait. Ce sens est encore marqué dans certains textes".
But, for his examples, the first is a misreading of Skene (see
III.29.ii); on the second, see note on II.3.iii, and below on *diriaid*;
for the third, cf. *Guledic deduit* above; for the rest, see on *diriaid*
below ("sage" is not antonym of "méchant" here). He is led
to this conclusion by his derivation from *do-ate* (or *eti*)-*uid+-*,
but this is by no means certain. It is difficult to give the true
meaning in one word; "fortunate" is perhaps the best, with
"prosperous" and "righteous" as occasional alternatives.

Dedwydd is not infrequently contrasted with *diriaid*, sometimes
with the sense "righteous", and evidently the two were regarded as
to some extent antonyms, e.g. Pen. 17 prov. 301, *gwell y am y paret a
detwid noc am y tan a dirieit*, "better by the wall with the righteous
than by the fire with the mischievous". The early meaning of
diriaid appears not to be "wicked" but rather "mischievous",
"wrong-headed", the perverse sort of person who is not really
vicious but who cannot help making a mess of things—a man born
under an unlucky star; see CLH, p.173. The best one word in
English is perhaps "mischievous".

V

ST.1. Englyn unodl cyrch. Note that a version of this stanza,
without l.iii, a pure milwr, occurs MA, 361 b.

l.i. **Kalan gaeaf**, signifies the actual day, the "Calends of
Winter", November 1st; Irish *samhain*, which however means
"end of summer". Tr. "Winter's Day", on the analogy of May
Day, New Year's Day; i.e. the day at the beginning of the season.
"Beginning of Winter" is too vague, and "All Saints' Day"
introduces ideas which do not belong to the phrase.

l.iii. Note the old form *no(c)*.

ST.2, l.i. *cyfrin*; now an adjective, but cf. VI.4.i, *gorwyn blaen
eithin a chyfrin a doeth*. The mutation is curious; is it influenced
by *kein gyfreu adar* below? "Winter's Day; fine is a secret shared";
there is no reason to tr. this line "On Winter's Day a secret
shared is fine", which would be a sufficiently foolish remark. The
phrase is a pure human-gnome, though certainly a nature-gnome
would be expected here.

Sᴛ.3, l.ii. **hauot**, an upland farmstead to which cattle are driven in the summer.

l.iii. **haed**, cf. PK, p.197. "Incurs."

Sᴛ.4, l.iii. *da6n*, "natural gift, talent". The usual form of the gnome is *lle ny bo dysc ny byd da6n*, as ɪɪɪ.27.iii. For this sense of *dawn* cf. DDG, p.54, 25, *annerch gennyd, wiwbryd wedd, Loyw ei dawn, leuad Wynedd*.

Sᴛ.5, l.iii, occurs also ᴠɪ.4.iii, RBH, 1056, 8, and Engl.Clyw. 17.iii. **Dewin** is here probably to be rendered "diviner", the usual meaning of the word, i.e. manticism is a false art and none knows the future but God, perhaps a hit at Giraldus' *awenyddion* and their like; but it might quite well be translated "There is no divinity but God", cf. *Cyuarchaf yr dewin gwertheuin gwerthuawr wrth y uod yn vrenhin*, MA, 198b, 18–19. *Un Duw, un dewin, un doeth*, Pen. 102, f.6. Note the *w* in *namwyn*, the old form even in RBH, where often *namyn*, e.g. ᴠɪ.4.iii.

Sᴛ.6, l.i. The mutation shows that *kein gyfreu* is a compound, "sweet-songed", predicative to *adar*. There is clearly a confusion in this verse, which as it stands describes partly a winter day— *Kalan gayaf...byrr dyd*, and partly a summer day—*kein gyfreu adar...ban cogeu*. The verse has got into the Kalan Gaeaf series from a summer series, probably a Gorwynion since it occurs in ᴠɪ.31, but *da6n goleu* in l.ii. The original form of the stanza is probably that in BBC, f.xʟɪɪ, *gorwin blaen pertheu, kein gywrev adar, hir dit, bann cogev; trugar daffar Duv orev*; an interesting piece of evidence that Gorwyn verses go back *at least* to the late twelfth century. **Cyfreu**="words, song", *not* "plumage"; cf. Loth, ACL, ɪ, p.469, "le sens habituel de cyfreu est paroles, ordinairement chantées, chant". See CLH, p.162.

l.iii. **daffar**, cf. ᴠɪ.33.iii. "Le mot signifie en effet clairement provisions, secours à la disposition de", Loth, ACL, ɪ, p.497. "The merciful providence of God is best"; hardly "merciful providence, God has made it", which would need the relative particle and infixed pronoun, *ae goreu*.

Sᴛ.7, l.i. **kalet cras** can hardly refer to Kalan Gaeaf as it is not regarded as a "parched" season in these poems, and analogy demands a self-contained gnome here.

l.ii. The usual form of this line is *purdu bran buan iyrchwyn* (or some other animal), e.g. ɪɪɪ.14.ii. And why is *govras* ("stout") mutated? But cf. *breit allan orseuir*, ɪ.2.iii, and *trugar daffar Duv orev*, BBC, f.xʟɪɪ. The explanation of the arrow from the bow (Skene) is fanciful. On this stanza, cf. a poem in Pen. 102, f.8, st.3, *calan gauaf, calaf cras, du plu bran, gnawd buan bras, am gwymp hen chwerddid gwen gwas*, "Winter's Day, the reeds are parched,

(55)

black is the plumage of the raven, usual for the stout to be swift",
etc., which confirms the interpretation of **ovras** and tempts one
to read *calaf cras* here.

St.8, l.i. **kerwyt**, fr. *carw*. A plural or collective termination?

l.iii. **gwir**=*ys gwir*? cf. 1.21.v, *breit guir orseuir allan*? and
MA, 140a, 18, *gwir gwae i werin gwin eu gwirawd*; cf. the same use
common in Irish, e.g. Pokorny, *A Historical Reader of Old Irish*
(Halle, 1923), p.9, *Fír, olse, ingen fil and 7 bid Deirdriu a ainm*,
"True, he said, it is a girl and Deirdre shall be her name". Or
should one read *gwir-well, gwir-wae*, like *iawndda*? Does *breit
guir* correspond to the complementary *da iawn*?

St.9, l.i. **godeith**=a bonfire, *not* "heath" (Strachan Introd.
p.261). Can it mean here the spot where the burning took place?
Cf. *beacon*, a signal fire but also the peak on which the fire was,
in place-names.

l.ii. Cf. *ereidir in rich ich i guet*, BBC, f.xvii.3 (where, however, the scene is early summer), and *ol6yn yn rhych ych yn y
6aith*, MA, 359a, 38.

VI

St.1, l.i. **gorwyn**. Skene "bright", but this does not always
apply very well. *Gwyn* can mean also "delightful", "happy",
cf. *gwynfa* and *gwyn ei fyd*, etc.; "delightful" fits all the cases
quite satisfactorily. *Gor-* is intensive here.

l.iii. "A heart full of longing leads to sickness." **Brong6ala**,
from *bron* and *gwala*, "fullness"; note the non-mutation of the *g*,
implying an exemplar of BBCh. date at latest.

Y heint, cf. Engl.Clyw. 25.iii, *pob hir letrat y groc*,
"long thieving leads to the gallows"; Bidiau 11.8.ii, *bid henaint
i dlodedd*, "old age leads to poverty".

St.2. The stanza is a variant of RBH, 1035, 3–4, which breaks up
a *gordyar adar* series and is perhaps out of place. The difference
in l.iii must be due to oral transmission, not scribal error.

l.ii. **keinmygir**, cf. *caín* in verbal compounds in Irish. The
meaning is certain but the root is difficult and the lack of mutation
curious; cf. *edmyg, dirmyg*, but *gofygu, keinfyg*.

Pob, cf. the identical use of *cach* in proverbs in Irish,
and *omnis* in mediaeval Latin, e.g. Gaselee, *An Anthology of
Mediaeval Latin* (Macmillan, 1925), p.78, "sic foris fertilis sed
intus sterilis omnis hypocrita" in a gnomic poem. The translation
"every skilful one is honoured", etc. is clumsy and not English;
the meaning of *X pob Y* is simply that the Y as a class are X.
Tr. "the skilful are honoured".

l.iii. The **heint** in question is presumably love-sickness.

Sᴛ.3, l.i. **eilic**, "brisk"? Cf. CLH, p.142. The word seems to mean "valiant, vigorous, swift", cf. *arial*, "vigour".

l.iii. Cf. *trech vyd anyan noc adysc*, Engl.Clyw. 31.iii; *trech annyan noc adysc*, WB prov. 213.

Sᴛ.4, l.i. **cyfrin**, see v.2.i, note.

l.ii. **disgethrin**, cf. *a dywa6t yn disgethrin anhygar 6rth Peredur*, WBM, 141, "and he said roughly and unkindly to Peredur". *Disgethrin*="asper, austerus", D.

l.iii. See v.5.iii, note.

Sᴛ.5, l.i. **meillyon**, Mod.W.="clover", but cf. *mellhionou*, gl. "violas", VVB, p.184. The original meaning seems perhaps to be "small meadow flowers".

Sᴛ.6, l.ii. Refers to l.iii, which is itself a reflection on **g6ythla6n eidic**.

l.iii. "It is the sensible man's task to love truly", or "it is a wise task"; but cf. 15.iii below, where the other arrangement is preferable.

Sᴛ.7, l.i. **anhuned**, "wakefulness, disquiet"; metaphorically used here.

Sᴛ.8, l.ii. "'There is froth on mead." **Cr6ybyr**; the meanings are "cloud, froth, scum, lees of honey, hoarfrost". Cf. *Gorwyn lliw crwybr ewyn crych*, "bright, the colour of the froth of rippling foam", J. C. Morrice, *Gruffudd ab Ieuan ab Llywelyn Vychan*, p.48. *Ar cr6ybren wen 'n yr awyr*, Cymmrodor, ɪᴠ, p.120; "An unregistered form which evidently means *cloud*", "...In parts of S. Wales it has another meaning, 'hoarfrost'", *ibid.* p.136 (Llanstephan 2, 222 reads *wybren wenn*). *Ibid.* p.120, *tr6y y cr6ybyr ymblayn ka6ad o'r gla6*, "the cloud before a shower of rain" (Llanstephan 2, 122, *gan wybren ymlaen diruawr gawat*). *Crwybr*="favus, faex mellis", D. Cf. RC, x, p.329. Cf. st.14, l.iii below.

l.iii. **whefris**, cf. st.13, l.ii, *wheueryd*. Cf. Bull. ɪᴠ, p.136. The verb and its forms are quite uncertain, though the meaning "happen" seems to suit. The second *e* in *wheueryd* seems to be superfluous but I do not emend because of this uncertainty; note the association with *gwall* in both cases.

Sᴛ.9, l.ii. **g6esgerit**, fr. *gwasgaru*. Note the double vowel-affection.

l.iii. **pell** in the sense of time, cf. CLH, p.106. **Y**=*yn*, followed by soft mutation, see PK, pp.102 and 122.

Sᴛ.10, l.iii. Cf. BBCh. prov. 47, WB prov. 188, Engl.Clyw. 35.iii.

Sᴛ.11, l.ii. **eiryoes**, cf. *eirioes*="formosus", Arch. Brit. 61. *Eirioes*="pulcher", D. *Eirian ne eirioes*, "tec, fayre", WS. *Yn eiryoes yn eiryan*, "fairly, splendidly", RBH, 1176, 33. *Eirioes coed*, "fair is the wood", MA, 146a, 2. *Eirioes y perthaist*, MA, 154b, 14, where it seems to be used as an adverb, = "finely". In *kyflaun y eiryoes*, MA, 162a, 3, it is used as a noun, as here, = "fair thing"; therefore *kat6et pa6b y eiryoes* = "let each guard what he considers a fair thing".

St.12, l.i. Note this early occurrence of the *ty dail* motif dear to the Cywyddwyr.

Kynnadyl, cf. *ef a gerd6ys parth a'y gynnadyl*, "he went to his rendezvous", WBM, 8.

l.ii. **bac6ya6c**, see II.1.i, note.

St.13, l.ii. **wheueryd**, see note to st.8, l.iii.

St.14, l.i. **dedwyd**, see IV.11.iii, note.

l.ii. **meryd**, see IV.5.i, note.

Mall, see Bull. III, p.56. "Wicked."

l.iii. **cr6ybyr**, see st.8, l.ii, note; here = "hoarfrost".

Carchara6r dall, according to the usual order of these gnomes, should mean "the prisoner is blind", perhaps because of the darkness of his prison; but "the blind man is a prisoner" gives so much better and more probable sense that it is the more likely rendering.

St.15, l.i. **Digoll bre**, cf. *ac y kych6ynnyssont…parth a chevyn Digoll, a g6edy eu dyuot hyt ym perued y ryt ar Hafren…*, WBM, 209; *Lluest Gatwalla6n…yg g6arthaf Digoll uynyd*, RBH, 1043, 23. "Cefn Digoll, the Welsh name formerly given to the Long Mountain or Mynydd Hir, south of Welshpool", ACL, III, p.51, s.v. *coll.*

l.ii. **ffoll**, see Bull. I, p.225, where IW shows *ffoll* = something like "bag", from Latin "follis". The idea is that the puffed-up wind-bag of a man has no worries.

l.iii. **g6eithret** seems to imply "deed suited to" or "proper for"; almost "duty". Cf. *g6na6n weithret g6r kyt byd6n g6as*, "I used to play a man's part though I was a youth", RBH, 1042, 2.

Aruoll, cf. LLJ, and Bull. I, pp.226–7; = "pledge".

St.16, l.i. **corsyd**; Mod.W. *corsydd* = "marshes", sg. *cors*; *corsen* = "reed", pl. *cyrs*. But see WG, p.219.

St.17, l.i. *menestyr* = "cupbearer"; the idea is that the reckless are their own cupbearers, i.e. continually pour out wine for themselves. Cf. *d6ylla6 (leg. dy6alla6) di, venestyr*, "pour out, cupbearer", MA, 191a, 7. Borrowed from Norman-French *menestre*.

St.19, l.i. **kym6yn** fr. *mwyn*, = (1) "gentle", (2) "wealth" (Irish *maoin*, "wealth, riches"), as in *Mwynfawr*. *Kymwynas* = "a kindness, a benefaction", Irish *comaoin*, "a favour, recompense", therefore *kymwyn* also = "profitable"?

l.iii. i.e. to have solicitude for one person only is scarcely worthy of the name. Cf. *amgeled am vn nydi6*, RBH, 1044, 39, evidently a variant, and the meaning is explained in the next englyn, *ny elwir coet o vn prenn*. See CLH, p.63.

St.20, l.i. **kada6arth**; occurs elsewhere only in *arall at6yn katawarth yn egin*, BT, p.9, 20. This is not sufficient evidence to prove the traditional translation "charlock", e.g. Hugh Davies, *Welsh Botanology*, gives *cadafarth*, "charlock", but only quotes these passages. *Cedowrach*, "burr", must be a different word.

　l.ii. "How the blind escape scandalisation!" **Diwarth**; *gwarth*="insult" or "scandalisation"; i.e. the blind cannot see the things which would cause them scandalisation, *gwarth*. But cf. *bit diwarth eirchyat*, Bidiau 1.16.i, i.e. the *gwarth* takes no effect upon him because he is so unshamable.

　l.iii. "Boys are nimble and grimy". **Mannawc**=*bannog*, "speckled, spotted, or horned". There is a confusion between two roots, *mann*, "a spot", and *bann*, "a peak", "horn", etc.; in *Elen Vanna6c* it is presumably "of the love-spot"; in the *vchen bannog* of Hu Gadarn it is either "dappled" or "horned".

St.21, l.i. **kyra6al**, now *criafol*, but the rhyme shows *-al* is the termination here, not *-aua6l*; see Bull. ii, p.298.

St.22. Metre milwr of 887, see Loth, MG, ii.1, p.186.

　l.i. **didar** fr. *tar* in *taran*, "noisy" and *trydar*, "noise"?

　l.ii. **geuvel**, cf. *dan y gvellt ae gvevel*, BBC, f.xxxiii.15, fr. *gwyw*, "withered", and the same *wel* or *fel* as in *poethwal*, *poethfel*. Cf. *gwyddwal*, "a thicket"?

St.23, l.i. Cf. *glyn teccaf o'r byt a g6yd gogyfuch ynda6*, WBM, 225, and *aghiid y guit*, "its trees of unequal height", BBC, f.xxvi.8.

St.24, l.i. *Berwi*; the idea is "to bubble" originally, and so "to boil". Note that the line is a syllable short. The scribal error in l.ii suggests the exemplar wrote *u* for *w*.

　l.iii. **g6nelit**. This appears to be a subjunctive stem with a present indicative ending; the form occurs elsewhere in these poems (though it seems not to be recognised in the grammars) and always in an indicative sense (e.g. st.28, l.iii, *g6nelit da diwyt gennat*=Engl.Clyw. 60.iii, *digawn da diwyt gennat*; cf. CLH, p.169); is it perhaps a relic of a time when the stem *gwnel-* was not confined to the subjunctive? Cf. on the stem *el-*, WG, p.367.

St.25, l.i. Something has gone wrong with the englyn. The temptation is to take *ac ereill* as an incorporated gloss = "and other sources have", i.e. that one source had *gorwyn blaen kelyn kalet* and others *gorwyn blaen kelyn, eur agoret*; but the first would be an exception to every other stanza in the poem by omitting a second gnome in the first line and by qualifying the plant; while the second would be one syllable too long even for the extended milwr of 877, and the meaning would be obscure. *Ac ereill eur-agoret* makes sense, and *kalet* looks like a contrast, with a noun lost; *angawr*, "miser", fits very well, making a penfyr, and if one could read *awr-agoret* (see Cymmrodor, XXVIII.178) would give internal rhyme (IW). Note that the gnome in l.iv occurs elsewhere (e.g. Engl.Clyw. 37.iii) without *pan gysco*, etc., which is perhaps an unnecessary accretion; or it may genuinely be due to a fusion of stanzas.

ST.26, l.i. **elwic**, cf. *torredic Eidic alaf elwic*, "of wealthy possessions", MA, 310a, 4. *Elw*="gain, profit". Cf. CLH, p.57.

l.ii. **deilyedic** formed from *deiliad*, "tenant", like *trevedic* from *trefad*, gl. "rusticus" and "colonus", Norris, *Cornish Drama*, II, p.422. The idea is that the rent-paying villein has a hard day's work. If fr. *dail*, "leaves", "the long day is leafy", i.e. a summer day, but this is unusually abstruse for the phrasing of these poems.

l.iii. **dirmic**, cf. Laws, p.21, *Ef bieu capaneu y brenhin...ae yspard6neu...pan dirmyccer*, "when they are discarded"; cf. also *ibid.* pp.24 and 27.

ST.27, ll.i and ii. Cf. *a phan edrych6yt y dyle, nyt oed arnei namyn byrwellt dysdlyt ch6einllyt a boneu g6rysc yn amyl tr6yda6, a g6edy ryussu o'r dinewyt y meint g6ellt a oed uch eu penneu ac is eu traet arnei*, WBM, 203. It shows that rushes, etc. were used for an inferior sort of bedding stuffing. WOP tr. ll. ii and iii, "When drawn under the pillow the wanton mind will be haughty" (!).

ST.28, l.i. **hwylyat**, cf. Irish *seól*, "a course".

l.iii. **g6nelit**, note the rhyme in *-yt* and see III.6.ii, note, and VI.24.iii, note.

Diwyt, Mod.W. "diligent", but cf. Bull. II, p.11, where="a man you can depend upon"; also RB.Brut, 128 and DDG, p.94, l.18, and *ibid.* p.154.

ST.29, l.i. **bydina6r**="one who likes to be in hosts"? LLJ takes it in this passage as pl. of *byddin*. Leg. *bydinawc*?

l.ii. **lla6r**, cf. *laur* gl. *solum* (VVB, p.172; it is *sōlus*, not *sŏlum*, IW.). *Tri vgein mlyned yt portheis i la6rwed*, "I suffered solitude", BT, p.19, 16. As a personal name and a common noun="champion" (i.e. monomachus?). The idea is here that when alone in a wood one hears birds, but a crowd drives them into silence.

ST.30, l.iii. **g6nelyt**, see st.28, l.iii, note.

ST.31. See v.6, note.

ST.32, l.i. The reading *erpein* of J suggests that its exemplar used here the Anglo-Saxon letter þ, =*w*. **Elein**, see RC, VIII, p.497. *Elain*="hinnulus, damula", D.

l.ii. **migyein**, see PK, p.211; cf. RBH, 1432, 8. Or, Pen. 76, 118, *chware mig*="play hide and seek behind the hand"; so in Mod.W. Cf. *g6rach vegyrwan vic*, "bent", RBH, 1337, 40.

Is the idea "bending", "hiding"? For the termination, plural, cf. *g6eissyonein*, double plural of *g6as*, RBH, 1038, 8. On the reading of J, *nugyein*, cf. *guatuaru y dan nugyaw y penneu arnau* (Hengwrt MS. 11.256, Pen.5 (Y Groglith)), "shaking their heads at him". "*Nug*, 'a shake', *nugiaw*, 'to shake, quiver', *nugiaw gan y cwn* (but *gan y cawn*, D. prov.), 'to be shaken by the dogs'", Pughe. Therefore "The trees are swaying"?

l.iii. "Intercession for one who is not loved does not prevail."
Eiryawl="intercede", D. The reading of J is supported by *eirya6l a gara6r ha6dweith*, "intercession for one who is loved is an easy task", RBH, 1056, 32. For the construction, cf. *a'm eiryolo Pedyr*, "May Peter intercede *for* me", RBH, 1151, 12. For the *-awr* termination=*present* tense, cf. *ch6erdyt bryt 6rth a gara6r* in st.29, l.iii.

Ny gyghein, fr. *cynghanu*, see T. Lewis, *Gloss. Med. Welsh Law*, s.v. *cyghanu*="to prevail", "obtain", "be legal".

St.33, l.iii. Can mean either "woe to him who has to take alms", or, in view of *dygit Duw dafar o law*, Pen. 17 prov. 225, ="God snatches provision out of the hand", it might be "Woe to him who snatches provision from the hand".

VII. (BIDIAU I)

On this poem and its relations to the following poem, see pp.9 ff. A few emendations have been made from the Peniarth and Addl. texts of Bidiau II and scattered gnomes in the Peniarth 17 list (see p.10) where the Red Book text positively demanded it and the others offered a probable solution; but this has been done very cautiously, and not for example in the case of pure oral variation. In editing, I call Peniarth 17 proverbs, PP; Peniarth 102, P; Addl. 14873, A; Panton 14, Pt; and Peniarth 27, P2.

St.1, l.i. **bit**. Strachan Introd. p.98 takes this as a "consuetudinal" present indicative. But see J. T. Morgan, Bulls. v and vi; he takes *bid* in the imperative sense to be "an expression of resolve", that is, "shall be, must be, needs to be"; but in the proverbs he allows the sense "is by nature", comparing A.S. *sceal* in gnomes. But on the contrary *sceal* in the Anglo-Saxon gnomes generally means "shall (be), should (be), must (be)", e.g. Exeter Gnomes, l.4, *God sceal mon aerest hergan*, "one shall praise God first"; l.49, *ne sceal hine mon cildgeonge forcweþan*, "one shall not rebuke him, young child as he is". "Is by nature" is expressed in the Anglo-Saxon gnomes by *biþ, byþ*; and *sceal* seems rather to have the force of "must needs be if it is to be at all"; so, Cotton Gnomes, l.i, *Cyning sceal rice healdan*, i.e. "a king, if he is to be a genuine king (cf. Welsh *teithiog*), must needs control the state".

Cf. Chadwick, *Growth of Literature*, I, pp.380 ff., where *sceal* is translated "is indispensable to", "is to be", "must be" (sometimes "is"); and so the Norse *skal* in gnomes is there tr. "is to be" (p.383, "the *skal* formula is the most common but *the present indicative also occurs*"). The same idea seems to be in the Welsh *bid* in gnomes, which is also the idea (as allowed by Morgan) elsewhere; thus *bid amlwg marchawg*, "the real knight needs to be conspicuous", "to have the *teithi* of a knight one must be conspicuous". "Shall be" or "should be" would perhaps express it most satisfactorily (Morgan compares, *op. cit.* p.32, "Ginger shall be hot in the mouth", i.e. "ginger is certainly hot, according to its nature"); *bid* then is something more than a simple present indicative, but "shall be" in this sense is not a generally intelligible modern English idiom, and it is perhaps best to translate "is". Note that *bid* frequently does not count in the scansion; cf. Loth, MG, II.2, pp.125 ff. Note the frequent mutation of the complement or the subject after *bid*; in Bidiau I there are about 78 per cent. of mutations to non-mutations, but in Bidiau II, which has been more modernised, only about 54 per cent. It is practically the rule for the complement to follow directly on the *bid* and before the subject; this is often quite clear, as *bit la6en meichyeit*, "joyful are the swineherds", but *bit anniweir annwadal* might be either "the fickle is faithless" or "the faithless is fickle"; unless it is quite clearly the contrary such cases are to be taken in the first way.

  Annyana6l, cf. Anc. Laws, I, p.222; II, pp.72, 206, where = something like "innate". RB.Brut 185, it tr. "innata" and "naturalis"; but cf. *greddf* = "strength" as well as "nature", and Bull. v, p.123, *pwy wyt, filwr anianawl*, where it must surely = "full of spirit". This meaning fits the context best here.

  l.ii. **buduga6l**, "triumphant, exultant", properly belongs to *llef* and is a violent case of transferred epithet. But cf. WBM, 488, *buduga6l y6 Bedwyr* = "skilled" or "gifted".

ST.2, l.i. WOP explains that the wind would shake the mast off the trees and so save the swineherds the trouble.

  l.ii. **teleit**, see III.11.iii, note.

  l.iii. **diryeit**, see IV.11.iii, note.

ST.3, l.i. **cuhudyat**, "accusing", cf. Laws, p.139, *maer cuhudyat*. A **keisiad** is one who comes to arrest, a beadle or catchpoll. **Cynifiat**, see III.19.ii, note.

  l.ii. "Clothes are well-fitting." P and A read *bid gynnwys gan dillad*, "the welcome goes with the clothes", the other meaning of *cynnwys*. The primary meaning is "to contain", from *condensus*.

ST.4. The emendation restores the rhyme in l.i and has the authority of P and A.

  l.i. *gavwy* = "avid, ardent"? Cf. ACL, I, p.449.

l.iii. **ar**, see WG, p.298.

Sт.5, l.ii. Cf. *seo sceal in eagan, snyttro in breostum*, "the pupil shall be in the eye, care in the breast", Ex. Gn. 123.

l.iii. **anniweir**, Mod.W. "lustful", but the early meaning is simply "unfaithful"; cf. the *trydyd anniweir teulu*.

Sт.7, l.iii. **deueirya6c**="deceitful", fr. *dau+gair*.

Sт.8, l.ii. i.e. after eating barley; cf. ὡς δ'ὅτε τις στατὸς ἵππος, ἀκοστήσας ἐπὶ φάτνῃ δεσμὸν ἀπορρήξας θείῃ πεδίοιο, *Iliad*, VI, 506–7.

l.iii. "(Even) gossamer presses upon grain in root"? I take this as a way of saying that even a light thing, actually or metaphorically, can be burdensome to the young or weak. Or leg. *g6isgyt* here and in the next stanza; "gossamer covers grain", etc.?

Sт.9, l.iii. **adneu**, see IV.1.i, note.

Sт.10, l.i. Cf. Pen. 17 prov. 118, *bit haha bydar*; 119, *bit anwadal ehut*. **Haha**="loud-laughing".

l.iii. "Happy is he on whom looks one who loves him." **Yr**. For the relative *ar* see WG, p.298, and for the confusion of *ar* and *yr* as prepositions see Bull. III, p.259. The Pen. 27 text of Bidiau II reads *ar* here.

Sт.11, l.i. **dyf6n**, RBH. Perhaps an error, but *dyfn* is used for *dwfn* in Gwynedd. But cf. Yst. Carl. Mag. p.4, l.22, *Kanys dyfwr a aeth drosti*, where leg. *dwfyr*.

Lynn, RBH. The emendation is confirmed by J, P, and A.

l.ii. *granclef* makes no sense; the P, A and PP readings show that RB and J are wrong. An exemplar *bit guarant leu gleu*, "the brave is a dependable lion", would account for all the forms; in which *u=w*, and PP read *t* as *c* and *u* once as *u*; P and A read *tl* as *d* and modernised *-eu* wrongly to *-au* in one case; and the common exemplar of RB and J missed *-wa-*, read *t* as *c*, and transcribed *-u* as *-f* once. It looks as if this was the stemma (see p.11):

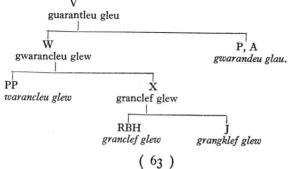

(63)

PP could not have been copying RBH, and the similarity of the mistake *c* and the correction *-ew* in both makes it look as if PP and X had a common intermediary between themselves and V. (For evidence of intermediaries between V and P, A, see p.11.) V must have been of BBCh. date at latest, since *u=w*. RB and J, which are close but independent texts, would scarcely both have miscopied *gwarancleu* so similarly; therefore a common exemplar X is postulated. (Professor Williams suggests *bit waran-cleu glew wrth awr*, with *waran=faran*, "the brave is quick to fury at the battle cry", or *bit waran-llew glew*, "the brave is of the fury of a lion", etc., cf. BA, p.15, 2, *lew mor hael baran-llew*. This would give (the more usual) mutation with *bit*, but it does not seem to account satisfactorily for the forms with *g-*; *waran-cleu* loses the internal rhyme, and *waran-llew* does not explain the *-cl-* and *-d-*.)

l.iii. *ma6r*, RB and J; an alteration by a scribe who did not understand "Irish" rhyme. Note that P and A have *nawdd*, but A seems to have started to write an *m* and to have finished by writing *nawdd*.

ST.12, l.i. **euein**, RB and J; P and A *eddain* (rhyming in *-in*). Cf. Pen. 17 prov. 115, *bit edein alldut*. See CLH, p.175. "Outcast" or "stranger" seems to fit satisfactorily; note that *eddain* is the better attested form. Etymology?

    Disgythrin, cf. VI.4.ii, note. Compare this stanza with Bidiau II.14 which is in a better state of preservation; it gives internal rhyme with *eithin* and *eddain* and *alltud* and *drud*, which this stanza does not, and introduces an additional gnome apart from the l.iii lost in RB. The verse has obviously suffered from oral transmission.

l.ii. **chwanna6c**="prone", "apt". Cf. Mod.W. *mae hi chwannog i law*, "it is prone to rain", "likely to rain".

ST.13, l.ii. **g6yn**; might be *g6yn*, "white", but the preponderance of mutations with *bid* and the evidence of P and A, *cwynfan*, supports *c6yn*. Note Pen. 17 prov. 123, *bit lawen yach*. Also the adjectival use of nouns in this verse and the next.

ST.14, l.i. **aele**; *aeleu* seems to be the same word; it is emended here for the rhyme with *aë*, but cf. RBH, 1048, 35, *onyt rac agheu ac aeleu*, where the *-eu* form is attested by rhyme. See D, "*aele*= gresyn, dolurus, tostur, trist, trwm".

    Aë. Meaning? See ACL, III, p.260, but it settles nothing. IW suggests read *re*, "an army is swift".

l.ii. *besgittor*, MSS., is no sense; *pesgittor*="is fattened". An adjective or noun is needed here, hence I read **basgadur**, but it is not an easy change scribally.

    Dyre "lascivia, libido", D. Noun=adjective here as elsewhere in the poem.

St.15, l.i. The sense shows that *vann*, the reading of RB, is correct; *wann* suggests an early exemplar with *v* spelt *w*.

l.ii. **hyuagyl**, fr. *magl*, Latin *macula*, "a stain, spot".

l.iii. See Bidiau II.12.iii, note.

St.16, l.i. "The suppliant is shameless."

l.ii. **reinyat**, cf. RC, XLII, p.372, note, where Loth derives it from *rhan* and makes = "distributor", therefore "prince"; cf. the Anglo-Saxon use of *beahgifa*, "ring-giver", etc., meaning "chief", "lord" (because the act of receiving gifts was an acknowledgment of dependence). Or derive from *rhain*, "stiff", and make it = "prop", "support". The translation "chief" perhaps combines both ideas. Cf. *etifedd Gwynedd gwanar gyrchiad neud Duw a'i rhannws yr hael reiniad*, MA, 222b, 31, where the connection appears to be with *rhan*; but *a chymot a'n rheen kynn no'n reinya6*, where *rhain* is better (RBH, 1193, 11).

Cyfarth. Loth, *loc. cit.*, tr. "celui qui distribue gronde naturellement", and takes *cyfarth* as "barking"; the regular meaning is the occasion when the hounds have brought their quarry to bay and surround it, barking; and the transferred meaning, as here, "battle"; cf. *dychyrch6ynt gyfarth mal arth o vynyd*, BT, p.16, 10–11; *llas arth yn y gyfarthfa* (var.), MA, 346a, 13; *Bran a gre yn y gyfarthfa*, *ibid.* l.41. (I read *cyfarth* following JGE, but am not satisfied that the true reading of RBH is not *cyfarch*, as in J.; which if correct would be an interesting case of the rhyme *ch* : *th* in Welsh, as in Irish.)

l.iii. Cf. Pen. 17 prov. 114.

St.18, l.i. *or6n*, MS., could be for *(g)6r6m*, a frequent spelling of *g6rm*, by an easy scribal confusion of *o* and *6*, = "harness is blue". **Gorun**, "noisy". Cf. *sychyn yg gorun en trydar*, BA, p.19, 9–10.

l.iii. **rygynga6c**, cf. Yst. Carl. Mag. p.63, l.14, *ar vul uchel rygynga6c*, "a tall ambling mule".

BIDIAU II

Where the text is the same as Bidiau I, refer there for notes.

St.1, l.iii. An exemplar *rad*, where *d* is a *c* with an accidental vertical stroke, would explain the variants, *r* being misread as *i*; P2 preserves the true reading.

St.3, l.i. **baglawg**, see II.1.i, note.

Rygyngawd, see Bidiau I.18.iii, note.

St.7, l.ii. "The ford is waded with the help of staves."

l.iii. **odwr**. Is this *godwr*, fr. *god*, "adulterous", with analogical loss of initial *g*? Note the variants; the scribes were puzzled.

St.8, l.ii. **i dlodedd**, see VI.1.iii, note.

Sᴛ.9, l.ii. See Bidiau 1.11.ii, note.

Sᴛ.10. The phrases seem disarranged and corrupted; there is no final rhyme in l.i, and the reading of Bidiau 1.2 is probably the correct one. L.ii, MSS. read *ar ei naid bid dedwydd*, but the rhyme should be in *-aid*, and the transposition is easy. **Naid** seems to have the same meaning as *nawdd*; "the fortunate is his own protection".

Sᴛ.12, l.iii. *lwytrew*, MSS., evidently taken by the exemplar of A and P for *llwydrew*, "hoarfrost", which makes no sense. Tr. "frost is grey".

Sᴛ.13, l.ii. **lleiniad**, fr. *llain*, "spear"?

IX

In editing I call Llanstephan 117, LL; Peniarth 99, P 99; Addl. 14885, A; Wrexham 1, W; Peniarth 111, P 111; and Cwrt Mawr 6, C.

Sᴛ.1, l.i. i.e. because of the many fires?

l.ii. **blin trulliad**, i.e. because there was more feasting in the long winter nights and so more work for him.

Trallawd klerddyn, "the wandering bard is sad", because of the bad weather he encountered in January? Note the use of noun as adjective, and cf. e.g. Bidiau 1.13.ii. Var. *treiglad*, "vagabond, roaming", *obambulator*, D.

l.iv. **buches**, "locus mulgendi vaccas", D.

Diwres, from *di* and *gwres*?

l.v. "Degraded is the man who is unworthy to be asked for anything." Note *i = ei*, the old spelling.

l.vi. Some explanation as that of st.2, l.v given in l.vi is needed.

Sᴛ.2, l.i. **ancwyn**, "secundae mensae, bellaria, dapes delicatiores", D; but cf. LLJ, s.v. *ancwyn*, and Bidiau II.8.iii. But Panton 1 gl. marg. "afalau ag aer[on], table fruit".

l.iii. **knawd** = *gnawd*; cf. the couplets *trem : drem, crau : grau*, by hardening.

Cysswyn; cf. "consensus, confoederatus, aliis cyffes; lladrad yn llaw neu lladrad *cysswyn*; *etifed cysswyn* filius qui clam acquiritur", D. "Acknowledgment" or "imputation"? D forces the meaning to fit his supposed derivation from *consensus*. Var. *cynllwyn*, "to dogge", S; "Insidiae, obsidiae", D; "to pursue", Lhuyd, Arch. Brit. p.215. Mod.W. = "plotting".

l.vii. **pen ki**. This is the commonest reading. LL has *pen kic*, P 99 and A *pen cil*. "A dog's head" seems to make no sense, nor does *penci*, "a dogfish". I follow Panton 1 gl. marg. "darn o fwa'r arch neu fwa'r cyfammod yn arwyddocau dirfawr ddry[cinoedd] a thymmestl", and take it to be a proverbial expression of ill omen and foreboding of storm. Was a rainbow on a spring morning considered a sign of bad weather?

St.3, l.i. **rhyfic**, "ambitio, arrogantia, insolentia, presumptio, superbia; a *myg*", D.

l.iii. **heiniar**, "proventus, peculium, fenum, penus, annona", D.

l.v. **arynaig**, cf. LLJ, s.v. *aryneic*.

St.4, l.iii. **clusthir**, i.e. the hare.

St.5, l.i. **difrodus**, "devastatus", D. *Difrawd*, "without regard", S. *Difrod*, "to deny", Lhuyd, Arch. Brit. p.216. "Wasting, extravagant, squandering, wasteful", SE. Does it refer here to the spring sowing?

l.iii. **diarchenad**, "lightly clad", because it is May and warm? See PK, p.105.

St.6, l.ii. **marianedd**. Note the variants; the scribes seem to have had difficulty with the word. A plural of *marian*="calculi, sabulum, sabura, locus sabulosus", D?

St.7, l.i. **hyglyd**, fr. *clyd*; or read *hyglud*, fr. *cludo*, "easily carried, ready for carting"?

l.vi. **kronffair**, "a small or petty fair"? SE, quoting this reference; but *crwn* does not mean "little", and "round" hardly fits here. Cf. Irish *cruinn*, "niggardly"? "No one visits a mean fair"?

St.8, l.i. **molwynoc**. Note the variants. Evidently the scribes did not know the word. "Plenus, ait LL.D.P. [Llyfr David Powell]", D. Cf. *Rhodri Molwynog*, "epithet not yet satisfactorily explained", Lloyd, *History of Wales*, I, p.231. But cf. also BBC, f.xxxiii.8–9, *Bet Meilir maluinauc saluvodauc sinhvir*, "Meilir the snail-like". Read therefore *malwenog* with C, and tr. "the salt-marsh is full of snails"?

l.iv. i.e. the greens have been turned into rickyards?

St.9, l.i. "There is verse in the Canon."

l.ii. "The ripening season of corn and fruit."

l.iii. Var. *g̊wyw*, "withered is my heart with longing" (cf. *g6y6 callon rac hiraeth*, RBH, 1035, 8) would perhaps give better sense.

l.iv. **tylodion**, var. of *tlodion*.

St.10, l.ii. **chwyrn**, "velox, pernix, celer, impiger", D.

St.11, l.i. "The fool grumbles."

l.ii. **llydnod**, cf. *llydnu*, "to foal".

St.12, l.v. **diddos**, properly, "not letting a drop (of rain) through", "weatherproof".

INDEX TO THE NOTES

INDEX

ADDENDA AND CORRIGENDA

P.3, n.1: Since published as *Studies in Early Celtic Nature Poetry* (Cambridge, 1935).

P.7, n.1: See *Studies in Early Celtic Nature Poetry*, pp.141ff.

P.8, l.6: But *llyvwr* occurs much later; e.g. *Ystoria de Carolo Magno* (ed. S. J. Williams), p.57, l.25.

P.8, l.9: But I am now very doubtful whether "Irish" rhyme can safely be treated as a dating criterion in popular poetry of this sort. I hope to publish detailed reasons for this elsewhere.

P.8, l.22: Note that what seems to be the same word occurs in the plural, *menestri*, already in the *Gwarchan Kynfelyn*; see Ifor Williams, *Canu Aneirin*, p.55, l.1404. Op. cit. p.372, Williams suggests an early Latin loanword *mynystr* or *mynestr* later influenced by Old French *menestre*, whence *menestr*; and that the form in *Gwarchan Kynfelyn* is a spelling for *mynystri*. In the present passage the internal rhyme with *elestyr* proves that we have here the later form, influenced by the French.

P.13, l.18: The *Englynion* were doubtless attributed to Aneirin chiefly because of his reputation as supposed author of the gnomic poem *Gwarchan Adebon*. Cf. Williams, *Canu Aneirin*, p.lviii.

P.14, l.24: Final *-f* in polysyllables was evidently being dropped in speech in early times; at least as early as the Book of Llandaff in the case of *-af*, and probably earlier. See my *Language and History in Early Britain*, pp.417f. Loss does not appear in rhyme in early poetry, but this is because it was regarded as a colloquialism. In fact there are certainly instances older than the 15th century; e.g. the Peniarth 3 text of Cyfoesi Myrddin, written *c*.1300, *bennaf | kredaf | para*, "will last" (Bull. IV, p.116); = RBH, col.581, ll.7–8. So RBH, col.1027, ll.5–7, *kyrhaedaf | kaffaf | yna* (the author's emendation, ZCP, XXI, 29 is probably unjustified). An early instance of *-af* in rhyme written as *-a*, but rhyming as *-af*, is RBH, col.582, ll.17–19, *dywedaf | disgoganaf | Kynda*, the name *Cyndaf* < *Cunotamos* (Peniarth 3 text *dywedaf | disgoganaf | Kyndaf*,

(71)

Bull. IV, p.118). The *cynghanedd* in Dafydd ap Gwilym often shows loss of *-f*, e.g. *Pa un o'r mil? Penna'r Mai* (T. Parry, *Gwaith Dafydd ap Gwilym*, no.23, l.38).

P.14, l.26: The *rhyme* of final *-aw(-)* in polysyllables with *-o(-)* may not be older than the 14th century, but the development to *-o(-)* had already taken place *in speech* by at least the 12th century; see my *Language and History in Early Britain*, §12, and especially p.298, middle. The rhyme of *-awr* with *-or* in the Books of Aneirin and Taliesin is noted by Ifor Williams (*Canu Aneirin*, p.351). These, however, must be very archaic and go back to the time when final *-aw(-)* in polysyllables was still *-ō(-)*, probably before the 8th century (see *Language and History*, §11).

P.43, st.3, l.iii: For *kedic*, LLJ gives *dicllon, llidiog, cythrublus*, and the *Geiriadur Prifysgol Cymru* adds *llym* to these. Note that Ifor Williams now suggests a stem *cad*, "strong", as in *cadarn*, for Cadnant (*Enwau Lleoedd*, p.41; = Cyfres Pobun, vol.v, Liverpool, 1945).
The comparisons with *blouc'h* and *blog* would need *in bluch* or *in wluch*, and *im* would be impossible. The reading of the MS., *ini*, is difficult to account for.

P.44, st.11, l.i: See a note on this passage by Vendryes, RC, XLVI, 314. He translates "Des mains d'or (i.e. généreuses) autour des coupes, des coupes autour des clercs", or "Des poignées d'or pour les coupes, des coupes pour les clercs." LLJ takes *clwyr* here as perhaps *mintai, torf*, "company", "host". We should perhaps translate "gold handles round drinking-horns, drinking-horns (circulating) round the company".

P.44, st.12, l.i: The sense "shelter" given by LLJ for *gogaur* suits the present context better.

P.44, st.12, l.ii: LLJ takes *diulith* here as negative of *gwlith*, but the sense seems not to suit very well, and the internal rhyme with *dit* is lost. Cf. st.14, l.3.

P.45, st.15, l.ii: See now LLJ, s.v. *cunlleið*, and *Geiriadur Prifysgol Cymru*, s.v. *cunllaith, cunllaidd*. These are guesses, and not very satisfactory ones, though they have the advantage of keeping the MS. readings.

P.45, st.16, l.ii: LLJ suggests "foam" for *emriv*, relating it to *briw*, which seems a rather unconvincing guess.

P.45, st.17, l.i: LLJ keeps the MS. reading and regards it as a compound of *methl*, rendering "deceitful, full of snares", which is perhaps preferable; "the watercourse is full of hidden pot-holes"?

P.45, st.17, l.ii: On *callet* see Ifor Williams, *Canu Aneirin*, p.331; LLJ, s.v. *calleð*; *Geiriadur Prifysgol Cymru*, s.v. *calledd*. A derivative of the same root as in *celli* rather than a plural of it. Perhaps "trees" or "herbage" here.

P.45, st.20, l.iii: Strachan takes *ry* here as "of possibility" (Ériu II, 61), but suggests as an alternative that *ry dieigc* might mean instead "is wont to escape", saying that this shade of meaning seems to be established for Irish (cf. Henry Lewis, Arch. Camb. XCI, 1936, p.163). Cf. now Thurneysen, *Grammar of Old Irish*, p.347f. The difference in meaning is rather slight in any case, and it is difficult to decide which is correct here.

P.46, st.1, l.i: The *Geiriadur Prifysgol Cymru* takes *baglawc* as "carrying spears", which is probably better.

P.47, st.1, l.ii: LLJ guesses "marvellously white", or perhaps "white-topped", as alternatives for *graenwynn*.

P.48, st.6, l.ii: But I had been misled by WG. As Henry Lewis notes in his review, Arch. Camb. XCI, 1936, p.163, what WG means is that the endings *-awd*, *-id*, and *-yd* can stand only in main clauses, not subordinate (or rather, in Irish terminology, can be only "absolute", not "conjunct"). *Chwerdit gwen gwas* here is of course a main clause, and would be "absolute" in Old Irish.

P.48, st.7, l.ii: Professor Thomas Jones translates "The fish (is) in the ford, its shelter is snug", with y = "his"; which is obviously right.

P.48, st.8, l.iv: The present writer, and apparently others, have inevitably taken *disgynnu* in the sense of "dismount", influenced by *ysgynnu* in the previous line which is certainly "mount". But a common early meaning is "to attack", "to charge" (cf. LLJ, p.372); and taking it in that sense here, *bar-ar-araf* may well be an adverbial phrase (with adverbial lenition) meaning "spear against weapon". That is to say, the chieftain charges with his spear and thrusts and parries the weapon of his opponent.

P.49, st.13, l.iii: Professor Thomas Jones translates "Bad eyesight makes a man a prisoner", which is certainly better.

P.49, st.19, l.i: LLJ's *caethiwydd*, or *caeth* etc., for *kynglhennyd* in this passage does not seem very happy. Cf. *Geiriadur Prifysgol Cymru*, s.v.

P.50, st.20, l.ii: The only evidence quoted by the *Geiriadur Prifysgol Cymru* for the sense "fine, adorned, flourishing" which it attributes to *bagwyog* is the present passage. This is scarcely good enough; it surely refers to the curly locks affected by the gentry, unlike the cropped head of the peasant.

P.50, st.25, l.iii: For $y = yn$ read "*y* is the equivalent of predicative *yn*". Professor Thomas Jones, who notes that *y* might also be "to" here, translates either "the brave man is a defender" (cf. LL.T, s.v. *erchwynn*) or "the brave man (goes) to the outer side of the bed". The first seems preferable.

P.51, st.32, l.ii: Cf. *bassaf dwuyr yn yt leveir*, Bull. IV, p.4.

P.52, st.5, l.i: On *y mro* see now Arwyn Watkins, Bull. XVII, pp.141ff. This spelling is common in M.W.

P.52, st.6: On the Book of Llywelyn Offeiriad see Henry Lewis, *Chewdlau Seith Doethon Rufein*, pp.21-2.

P.52, st.8, l.i: For *anllwyth* the *Geiriadur Prifysgol Cymru* follows LLJ in conjecturing that it is a compound of *llwyth*, "load", therefore "great load"; or a form of *anlloeth* in the sense of "tide, flood". In the context the second seems surely more probable. Silvan Evans reads *a thanllwyth* here, s.v. *cynllaith*, but does not quote his MS. source. LLJ takes *cynnlleith* in this passage as the same as *cunlleith* "battle, slaughter", and so does the *Geiriadur Prifysgol Cymru*. But this would appear to be the only instance of *cunlleith* so spelt; the alternation of *cun-* and *cyn-* is inexplicable; and the meaning does not appear to fit the context. Silvan Evans gives "humid, moist" as the meaning of adjectival *cynllaith*, but his only example is the present passage. The *Geiriadur Prifysgol Cymru* has *cynllaith* "bland, gentle, kindly, mild, calm; courteous, flattering, soft", identifying it with *canllaith*. Did Silvan Evans get his meaning from these senses? Translate, "usual is a day of flood in a mild winter"?

P.52, st.8, l.ii: LLJ gives *ffraeth, llafar,* for *kynrwytieith; Geiriadur Prifysgol Cymru* "free of speech, loquacious", while suggesting the reading *cyurwytieith,* i.e. *cyfrwydd-iaith.* The word appears to occur only here.

P.53, st.11, l.ii: LLJ renders *gorwyd* as *ael, ymyl, neu oror coed; llethr, llechwedd, neu fron coediog,* taking it as a compound of *gwydd* "wood".

P.54, l.12: For *do-ate* etc. read **do-ate-* (or *eti-*) *uid-.*

P.54, poem V, st.1: On *kalan gaeaf,* for "*samhain,* which however means 'end of summer' " read "*samhain,* the original meaning of which was 'end of summer' ".

P.55, st.3, l.ii: The point of the gnome *gwedw hauot* is that the animals were driven down from the hills to winter quarters *on* November 1st.

P.55, st.5, l.iii: Cf. T. H. Parry-Williams, *Canu Rhydd Cynnar,* p.294, l.75, *onid Tuw nid oes feddig.*

P.55, st.7, l.i: The suggested emendation *calaf cras* is perhaps supported by *Geiriadur Prifysgol Cymru, cras* as noun = "dry reeds or haulms". But Professor Thomas Jones suggests that *kalet* may mean *calledd* (cf. p.45, st.17, l.ii) and translates "the stalks (or reeds) are hard".

P.55, st.7, l.ii: Professor Thomas Jones emends *ovras* to *evras,* therefore "the 'perfect' man is nimble", i.e. the man whose physical powers are unimpaired. Cf. LLJ, s.v. This is a happy solution of a difficult passage; though the reading of Pen. 102 seems to support *govras.*

P.56, st.8, l.iii: Cf. Mod. Breton *gwir-wella,* "truly best"; RC, IV, 469.

P.57, st.3, l.i: See also now LLJ, s.v. *geilic.*

P.57, st.8, l.iii: LLJ suggests "wild, rough", s.v. *chwefris,* followed by *Geiriadur Prifysgol Cymru.* This is a guess for the present passage.

P.57, st.9, l.iii: But *y'm* is of course normal M.W. for "in my".

P.57, st.11, l.ii: On *eiryoes* see now LLJ, s.v.; and translate "let everyone keep his faith".

P.58, st.15, l.ii: Or *ffoll* = simply "dull, stupid"; therefore "the stupid man is care-free".

P.58, st.17, l.i: *menestyr*, see now the Addendum to p.8, l.22.

P.58, st.19, l.i: *kymwyn* may be "fruitful, prolific" here; cf. LLJ, s.v.

P.59, l.4 of the note on st.24, l.iii: Add "st.30, l.iii, *gwynelyt agheluydyt annerth*". Cf. Lewis and Pedersen, *Concise Comparative Celtic Grammar*, p.336, who note the indicative force of *gwnelit*. The meaning is "is wont to make, cause".

P.60, st.26, l.ii: LLJ seems to prefer "captured"; if so, "the captive, the slave, has a long day".

P.60, st.29, l.ii: For further instances see Ifor Williams in Bull. v, p.5.

P.61, st.32, l.iii: Professor Thomas Jones translates: "The intercession of one who is not loved does not avail"; which is preferable.

P.63, st.9, l.i: The sense of *bit trôm keu* is very unsatisfactory. Professor Thomas Jones makes the ingenious and convincing proposal that we should read *bit trôm bydar*, *bit grôm keu*, "A deaf person is hard of hearing, a hollow thing is concave"; noting the idiom *trwm ei glyw*, "hard of hearing".

P.63, st.10, l.i: Henry Lewis suggests rather that *haha* expresses "a request for a repetition of what has been said—'Eh, eh?'" (Arch. Camb. XCI, 1936, p.163). "Loud-laughing" was proposed because of the well-known fact that deaf people often talk louder than they need; but Lewis' suggestion is doubtless better.

P.63, st.10, l.iii: Henry Lewis kindly notes in a letter that *ae* may be taken here as the archaic form of the relative pronoun (O.W. *hai*); therefore "happy is he who sees whom he loves". The failure to mark lenition in *gôyl* and *kar* would in that case be archaic also.

P.63, st.11, l.ii: LLJ proposes to read *bit warancleu glew*, and takes *gwarancleu* as a compound of a hypothetical verb *gwaranc*, supposed to be cognate with Irish *fo-ro-icc*; to which he assigns the meanings "get, discover; reception, welcome". The second element he takes as *cleu* "quick", and he renders the whole as "easy to find". Therefore, "to the fore when the battle-cry is raised"? Alternatively he suggests the second element may be *llef*—"shouting a welcome to the battle-cry", which seems a little strained. The only example of the supposed *gwaranc* is this passage itself, which can scarcely be considered very satisfactory, and the explanation appears to me forced. It is true of course that internal rhyme with *glew* is not *necessary*, but in the circumstances it must surely be rather probable, especially as there are other instances of such internal rhyme in these poems (e.g. III.7.ii, V.7.ii, v.8.ii, VI.14.ii, and others). It is partly a question of method; which does the more violence, to emend *c* to *t* and interpret *u* as = *w*, or to invent a new verb which has no parallel anywhere in Brittonic, for the sake of this passage alone? The same might be said of some other instances in LLJ. I still prefer *gwarantlew*.

P.64, st.12, l.i: On *euein* see LLJ, s.v. *eðein*. It would be better to read *edein* here; *euein* is an instance of the sporadic interchange of *ð* and *v*. (In the note on p.64, for "note that *eddain* is", etc., read "note that *eddein* is", etc.)

P.64, st.14, l.i: *aele* and *aeleu* appear to be two different words, "sad" and "suffering" respectively; cf. LLJ and *Geiriadur Prifysgol Cymru*, s.vv. LLJ attempts to solve the difficult *ae* by reading *bit diaspat aeleu, bit ae[le] bydin* ("suffering is full of outcries, an army is sad", or the like), which is ingenious and metrically satisfying; but the point of the second gnome is then not obvious.

P.65, st.18 l.i: LLJ likewise takes the *or6n* of the MSS. as = *gorun*; cf. RBH, 1431.19, *gor6n*. Professor Thomas Jones prefers to keep *orwm*, = "blue".

P.65, st.7, l.iii: LLJ confirms *odwr* = *godwr*.

P.66, st.10: For "final rhyme" in the note on p.66 read "internal rhyme"; i.e. no rhyme with *meichiaid* (and *naid, ddiriaid*) before the *gair cyrch*. Delete the note on *naid*, and substitute "*naid* = 'good luck, fortune'; 'the fortunate is his own good luck'". Cf. CLH, pp.124–5. (I owe this reference to Professor Thomas Jones.)

P.66, st.1, l.vi: *garo i* scans as *garoi*; or read *gar* with LL and A. The *tri gelyn* are perhaps the world, the flesh, and the Devil? Cf. T. H. Parry-Williams, *Canu Rhydd Cynnar*, p.291, l.63, *gwae ni ochelo i dri gelyn* (likewise unexplained).

P.66, st.2, l.i: The meaning "fruit" or "dessert" for *ancwyn* suits the context best. See *Geiriadur Prifysgol Cymru*, s.v.

P.66, st.2, l.iii: On *cysswyn* see now LLJ and *Geiriadur Prifysgol Cymru*, s.v. For ' "Acknowledgment" or "imputation"?' in the note read "Accusation, insinuation".

P.67, st.3, l.vi is hypermetric; read *edn edwyn*?

P.67, st.5, l.viii is hypermetric; read *chroen davad*? But in these and other hypermetric lines in this poem we should remember that some were no doubt well-known prose proverbs, which perhaps the poet did not attempt to force into exactly seven syllables.

P.67, st.7, l.vi: *Geiriadur Prifysgol Cymru* gives "not large, comparatively small", and "young, small", among the many meanings of *crwn*; but "not large, comparatively small" is not illustrated by any of the examples quoted there, and the sense "young, small" seems to be applied only to children.

P.67, st.8, l.vi appears hypermetric; but scan *iddoi* or cf. the addendum on st.5, l.viii. In the poem *Helfa Hawdd ei Hepgor*, in which the lines normally have eight syllables, the proverb occurs as *y dyn ni weithia* / *ni fydd teilwng yddo y fara* (Parry-Williams, *Canu Rhydd Cynnar*, p.260, ll.137–8). This may be scanned by taking it as *yddoy* (or by reading *nid*; cf. the *ni bydd* of LL in the present passage).

P.67, st.9, l.iii: Cf. *Canu Rhydd Cynnar*, p.294, l.87, *gwae fy nghalon rrag hiraeth*.

P.67, st.9, l.iv: The number of syllables is correct; *tylodion* for *tlodion* is a genuine form, scanning as three syllables; cf. Lewis and Pedersen, *Concise Comparative Celtic Grammar*, p.94. There is therefore no need to follow A in reading *dyledion* (which gives poor sense and would in any case be spelt *ddyledion* in W, the basic text).

P.67, st.9, l.viii: Read *a ddiva 'r etifeddion* for metre.

P.67, st.10, l.vii: Scan *angaui* for metre.

P.67, st.11, l.ii: On *llydnod* cf. Bull. IX, p.320.

P.67, st.11, l.vi is hypermetric as emended; read *yr hael ai rhydd pieifydd*? See the variant readings.

P.69: Correct 55 in "*guir*, 'true', 45, 55" to 56; and add "*gwir*, 56" between *gwic* and *g6nelit*.

REPRINTED LITHOGRAPHICALLY IN GREAT BRITAIN
AT THE UNIVERSITY PRESS, OXFORD
BY VIVIAN RIDLER
PRINTER TO THE UNIVERSITY